HEREFORD TO NEWPORT
via Caerleon

Vic Mitchell and Keith Smith

Middleton Press

Cover picture: A northbound freight passes through Pontrilas in May 1950, hauled by 2-6-0 no. 5377. The junction signals are for the Golden Valley line to Hay. (Nelson coll./T.Walsh)

Published May 2005

ISBN 1 90447454 3

© Middleton Press, 2005

Design Deborah Esher

Published by
        Middleton Press
        Easebourne Lane
        Midhurst, West Sussex
        GU29 9AZ
Tel: 01730 813169
Fax: 01730 812601
Email: info@middletonpress.co.uk
www.middletonpress.co.uk

Printed & bound by Biddles Ltd, Kings Lynn

INDEX

56	Abergavenny Junction	80	Little Mill Junction	76	Penpergwm
65	Abergavenny Monmouth Road	100	Llantarnam	104	Ponthir
105	Caerleon	49	Llanvihangel	37	Pontrilas
99	Cwmbran	98	Lower Pontnewydd	83	Pontypool Road
7	Hereford - Barrs Court	78	Nantyderry	25	Tram Inn
1	Hereford - Barton	111	Newport	32	St. Devereux
		45	Pandy		

ACKNOWLEDGEMENTS

We are very grateful for the assistance received from many of those mentioned in the credits, also to A.C.Carder, R.Caston, L.Crosier, G.Croughton, M.Dart, F.Jeanes, E,Hancock, N.Langridge, B.W.Leslie, B.Lewis, C.Maggs, Mr D. and Dr S.Salter, N.Sprinks, P.Q.Treloar, M.Turvey, Dr R.W.Willé and in particular our ever supportive wives, Barbara Mitchell and Janet Smith.

I. Railway Clearing House map for 1947.

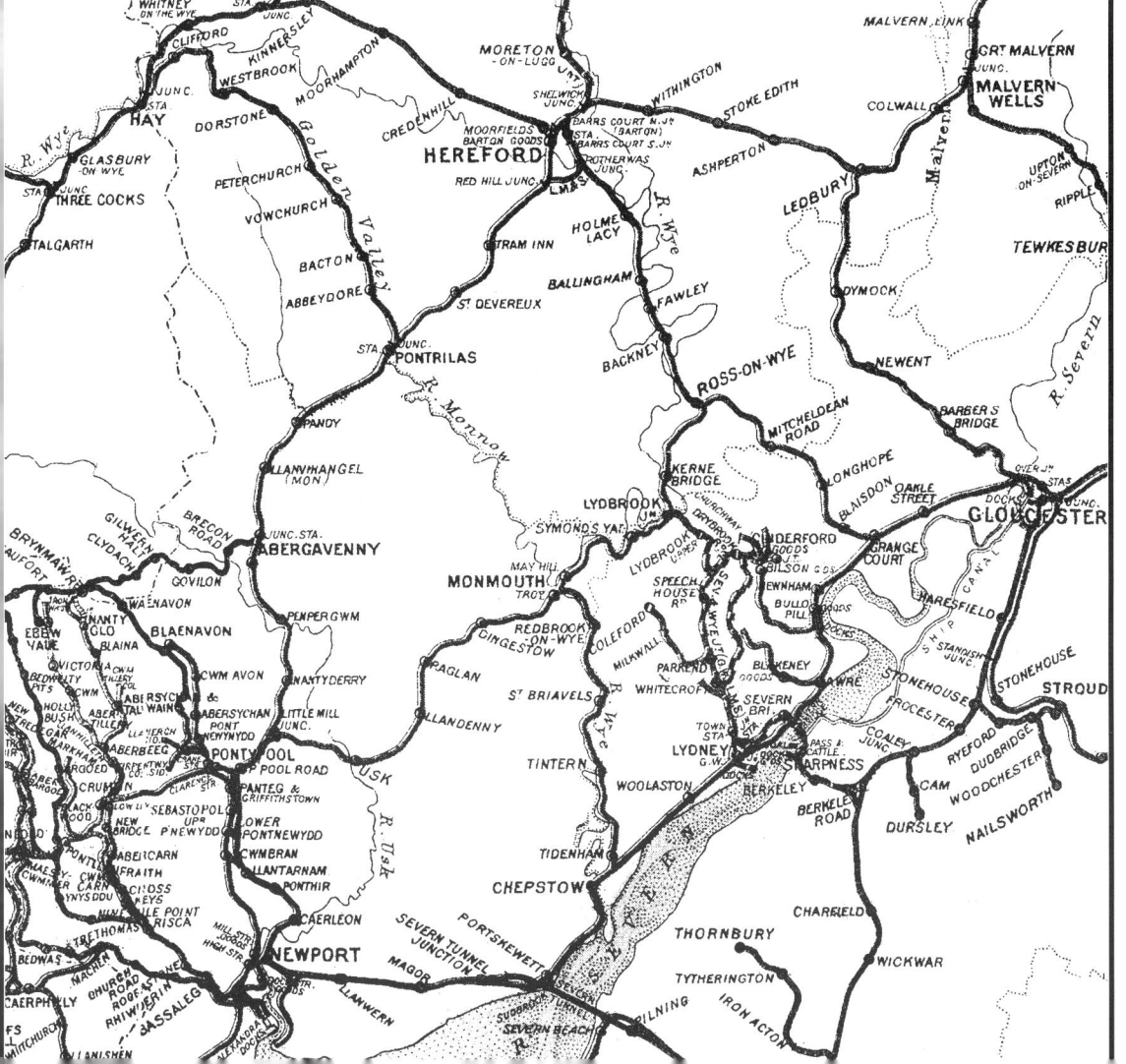

GEOGRAPHICAL SETTING

Situated near the confluence of the River Wye and River Lugg, the historic cathedral city of Hereford has for long been an important trading centre. Our route climbs gently out of the Wye Valley and runs over Lower Red Sandstones for most of its length.

South of Pontrilas, the line climbs steeply up the Monnow Valley for six miles to a summit at Llanvihangel. It then drops for seven miles and enters the Usk Valley near Abergavenny.

An undulating course follows until the route comes into the valley of the Afon Llwyd, near Pontypool. This river is a tributary of the Usk, close to which the line runs in its final two miles. This mighty river, along with the Ebbw River, gave rise to the creation of Newport as a place of great maritime importance in the 19th century.

The maps are to the scale of 25ins to 1 mile, with north at the top, unless otherwise indicated.

II. Gradient profile

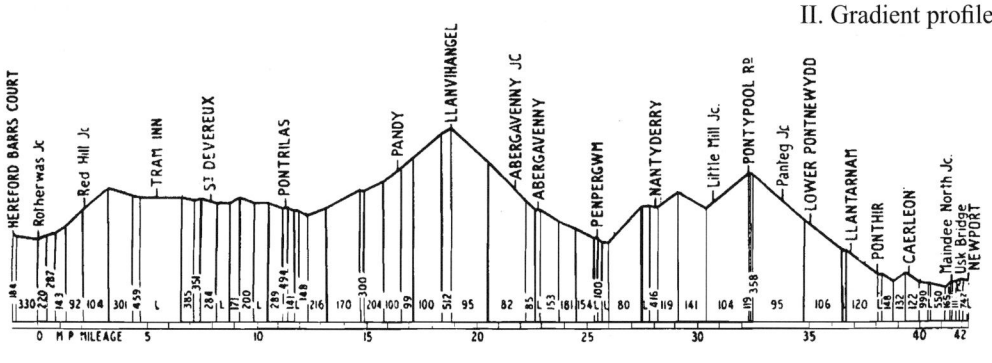

HISTORICAL BACKGROUND

The first goods transport system in the area comprised canals with feeder railways all worked by horses. The Monmouthshire Canal was completed to Govilon (west of Abergavenny) in 1799 and it joined the Brecknock & Abergavenny Canal, which was finished in 1812. Running northeast from near their junction was the 3ft 6ins Llanvihangel Railway of 1814; this joined the Grosmont Railway of 1820-21 at Llanvihangel. This in turn linked with the Hereford Railway of 1829 at Pontrilas.

The Newport, Abergavenny & Hereford Railway Act was passed in 1846 and the three railways mentioned above closed on 30th November 1852, as the new line was to run nearby or on their routes. It was laid to standard gauge and opened on 23rd December 1853 to a terminus at Barton, west of Hereford's city centre. The first station in Hereford was at Barrs Court, east of the latter, and it was the terminus of the 1853 Shrewsbury & Hereford Railway. This came into the joint ownership of the Great Western and London & North Western Railways, whereas the NA&HR passed into the hands of the West Midlands Railway in 1860, this in turn becoming part of the GWR in 1863.

The South Wales Railway's Chepstow-Newport-Swansea section opened in 1850, but was broad gauge. It came under GWR control in 1863 and was converted to standard gauge in 1872.

The Monmouthshire Railway & Canal Company opened a single line between Newport and Pontypool on 1st July 1852. The roughly parallel route between these places via Caerleon was opened for passengers by the GWR on 21st December 1874, this giving direct access to its Newport High Street station. The former route closed to freight in 1963.

The Hereford, Ross & Gloucester Railway opened in 1855, passenger service lasting until 1964. The Midland Railway-worked route west from Hereford opened partially in 1863. It lasted until 1962 for passengers.

Our route had other connecting lines: Pontypool to Crumlin (1855 to 1964), Pontrilas to Hay (1889 to 1941), Abergavenny to Brynmawr (1862 to 1958) and Little Mill Junction to Monmouth (1856-57 to 1955). The dates are for passenger services. Details of other links are given under the appropriate maps and closures of individual stations are stated in the captions.

Upon nationalisation in 1948, the route became part of the Western Region of British Railways. Privatisation in 1996 resulted in South Wales & West providing services ("South" was dropped in 1998). However, after reorganisation in 2001, Wales & Borders became the franchisee. Arriva Trains Wales took over in December 2003.

South of Hereford's Barton station, the three-arch Hunderton Bridge was built over the River Wye. It was reconstructed to a similar design in 1913, having carried a regular passenger service for less than 20 years. The structure was acquired by Hereford City Council in 1964, since which time it has carried only pedestrians and cyclists. In times of flood it has also been used by emergency vehicles. (Illustrated London News)

PASSENGER SERVICES

We will consider those in the down direction at about 20 year intervals, weekdays only initially, and not mention those running less than five days per week. The initial service comprised five trains, weekdays only, but from March 1854 there were only four.

The December 1870 timetable showed five departures from Hereford (all from Barrs Court), three calling at all stations, plus one extra south from Pontypool Road.

By 1890, there were ten leaving from Hereford and 14 arrivals at Newport; four were all stations. Three carried portions for Cardiff and Bristol or beyond, some originating at Birkenhead or even Glasgow.

The 1910 issue was complicated by some stopping trains terminating or starting at Pontypool Road or Abergavenny. There were 12 expresses of which four were North to West services.

The 1930 offerings were similar, but there were five through stopping trains. There had been major alterations during World War I.

A World War II extract from May 1944 features only two North to West trains (one with Manchester to Plymouth and Liverpool to Cardiff coaches) amongst the nine expresses. There were only three all-stations services.

A post-war revival followed, but the 1959 timetable following mass station closure had only one all-stations train (6.30am from Hereford) plus 15 others, three of which ran via the Severn Tunnel.

After ten years of cuts, the May 1969 issue contained just six departures from Hereford for Newport. Subsequent revival brought 24 arrivals at Newport in the 1989 timetable, five of which started at Abergavenny. A similar service was provided in 2005, but there were only two short workings.

Sunday services have varied greatly. From 1854 there were two departures from Hereford; similarly in 1870, when one was all-stations to Pontypool Road and one was likewise to Newport. By 1890, there was a 3.40am with one stop and a 7.50pm all-stations.

The 1910 timetable offered five expresses and by 1930 there were three expresses, plus a semi-fast. In 1944, four expresses were available. The 1959 timetable showed eight, plus a Liverpool to Plymouth train.

In 1969, all Sunday trains were at night, but since the 1980s there have been 9 or 10 trips on offer, well spaced.

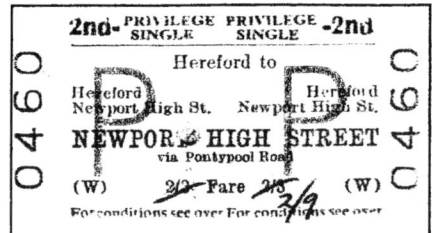

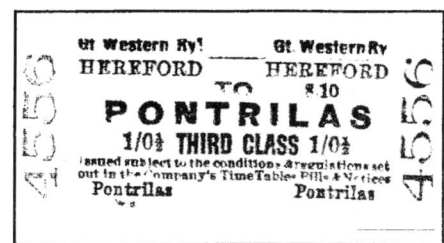

NORTH OF ENGLAND AND SOUTH WALES AND WEST OF ENGLAND
VIA HEREFORD

SATURDAYS ONLY

	pm	pm	pm	pm B	night	night	night
LIVERPOOL (Lime St.) ..dep	10 10	10J10	10P10	11 35	..	11 45	12 10
MANCHESTER (Lon. Rd.) „	10 27	11 15	11L15	11V15	12 15	11 55	12 35
Crewe .. .. „	11 39	11J39	11P39	12 45	..	1 25	2 0
Liverpool (Central L.L.) ¶..dep	....	....	10 55	10 55	10 55	10 55	10 55
Birkenhead (Woodside) .. „	....	....	11 10	11 10	11 10	11 10	11 10
Chester (General) .... „	....	....	12 10	12 10	12 10	12 10	12 10
Wrexham General .. „	....	....	12 38	12 38	12 38	12 38	12 38
	am	am	am	am	am	am	am
Shrewsbury ....dep	12 38	1 8	1 28	1 45	58	2 22	2 55
Hereford .. — — — {arr	....	2 17	2 37	2 53	3 5	....	4 0
dep	....	2 24	2 44	3 0	3 13	pp	4 15
Pontypool Road. .. .. ..arr	2 40	3 15	3 35	3 50	4 4	....	..
Pontypool Road........dep	....	....	....	....	....	4 45	..
Newport .. ..arr	....	....	....	....	....	5 12	..
CARDIFF (General).... „	....	....	....	....	....	7 25	..
Swansea (High Street) .. „	....	....	....	....	....	....	..
Pontypool Road..........dep	2 45	3 20	3 40	3 55	4 10	....	..
BRISTOL {Stapleton Road arr	....	....	....	....	....	....	6 5
Temple Meads „	3 52	4 32	....	5 20	....	....	..
	am	am	am	am	am		am
Bristol (Temple Meads).. ..dep	4 0	4 35	....	6 30	....	....	6 45
Taunton ....arr	5 5	....	6 15	7 50	7 30	....	8 5
Exeter (St. David's).. — „	5 51	....	7 5	8 50	8 20	....	9 0
Torquay .... „	7D10	....	8 25	9 50	9 25	....	10M52
Plymouth (North Road).. .. „	7 50	8 20	....	10 30	....	....	10 45
PENZANCE..........	11 30	11 30	....	1§50	....	....	....

SATURDAYS ONLY—continued

	am	am	am	am	am	am	am
LIVERPOOL (Lime St.)..dep	8 0	8 45	..	..	9 15	9 15	..
MANCHESTER (Lon. Rd.) „	8 10	....	....	9 10	9 25	....	..
Crewe .. .. „	9 16	9 50	....	....	10 30	10 40	..
Liverpool (Central L.L.) ¶..dep	7 25	8 45	8 55	8U55	....	9 15	9 15
Birkenhead (Woodside) .. „	7 35	8 55	9 5	9U 5	....	9 30	9 30
Chester (General) .... „	8 16	9 32	9 46	9 46	....	10 10	10 10
Wrexham General .. „	8 38	9 53	10 7	10U 7	....	10 30	10 30
	am	am	am	am	pm	am	pm
Shrewsbury ....dep	10 15	10 50	11 3	11 16	12 44	11 45	1 5
Hereford .. — — — {arr	11 25	12 2	....	12 27	12 47	12 57	1 17
dep	11 30	12 7	1 6	12 30	1 5	1 5	1 26
Pontypool Road. .. .. ..arr	12 22	12 59	....	1 25	1 39	2 0	2 20
Pontypool Road........dep	12 40	....	1 18	1 30	1 42	2F25	2 25
Newport .. ..arr	12 56	....	1 38	....	2 3	2F57	2 57
CARDIFF (General).... „	1 16	....	2 0	....	2 26	3F26	3 26
Swansea (High Street) .. „	3M11	....	3 18	....	3 50	5Z 2	5Z 2
Pontypool Road..........dep	12 25	1 0	1 10	1 30	....	2 5	2 25
BRISTOL {Stapleton Road arr	1 40	....	2 19	2 30	....	3 9	2 57
Temple Meads „	1 52	2 21	2 27	2 40	....	3 25	..
	pm	pm	pm	pm		pm	
Bristol (Temple Meads).. ..dep	2 5	2 25	2 35	2 50	....	3 35	..
Taunton ....arr	....	....	....	3 51	....	4 37	..
Exeter (St. David's).. — „	3 55	4 8	4 15	4 33	....	5 25	..
Torquay .... „	5 7	5 22	5 37	5 37	....	6 39	..
Plymouth (North Road).. .. „	5 55	6 20	6 30	....	....	7 30	..
PENZANCE..........	8 55	9 30	9 55	....	....	10 55	..

B Through Carriages Manchester to Penzance on 16th/17th September only
D Commencing 20th August arr 7 56 am
F Commences 2nd July. On 18th and 25th June dep Pontypool Road 2 52 pm and arr Newport 3 14 pm and Cardiff (General) 3 36 pm
I On 18th and 25th June and 17th September arr 3 18 pm
J Applies 24th June to 2nd September inclusive only
K On Saturdays 23rd July to 6th August inclusive arr 10 28 am
L Victoria Station, Manchester
P Commences 24th June
pp Calls at 4 25 am to set down passengers only
RC Refreshment Car
TC Through Carriages
U On Saturdays 2nd July to 27th August inclusive dep Liverpool (Central L.L.) 9 5 am, Birkenhead (Woodside) 9 20 am and Wrexham (General) 10 19 am
V On 16th September only
Z Via Aberdare (Pontypool Road dep 2 25 pm)
§ pm
¶ Change at Rock Ferry

PASSENGERS SHOULD ASCERTAIN IF CHANGE OF TRAIN IS NECESSARY

Summary of North to West trains via Hereford on Saturday mornings in the Summer of 1955.

HEREFORD - BARTON

1. The station was south of Eign Street and is seen in 1870 in the presence of MR 2-4-0 no. 55 of 1863. The main building was on the east side of the main line and was demolished in 1913. (GWR Magazine)

III. The 1947 edition at 1ins to 1 mile has the 1853 route from Shrewsbury at the top centre, the ex-MR line to Hay top left, the former broad gauge route to Gloucester lower right and our tracks to Newport lower left. The link line between the latter two is marked LM&SR and was opened by the LNWR in August 1866 to encourage Newport services to use Barrs Court station. At its east end is Rotherwas Junction and north of that is Hereford's station, once known as Barrs Court. The west end is at Red Hill Junction and north of that was Barton station. This closed to passengers in 1893 and is shown in detail on the next map. It ceased to be on a through route in 1966, but freight continued north of it until 1979.

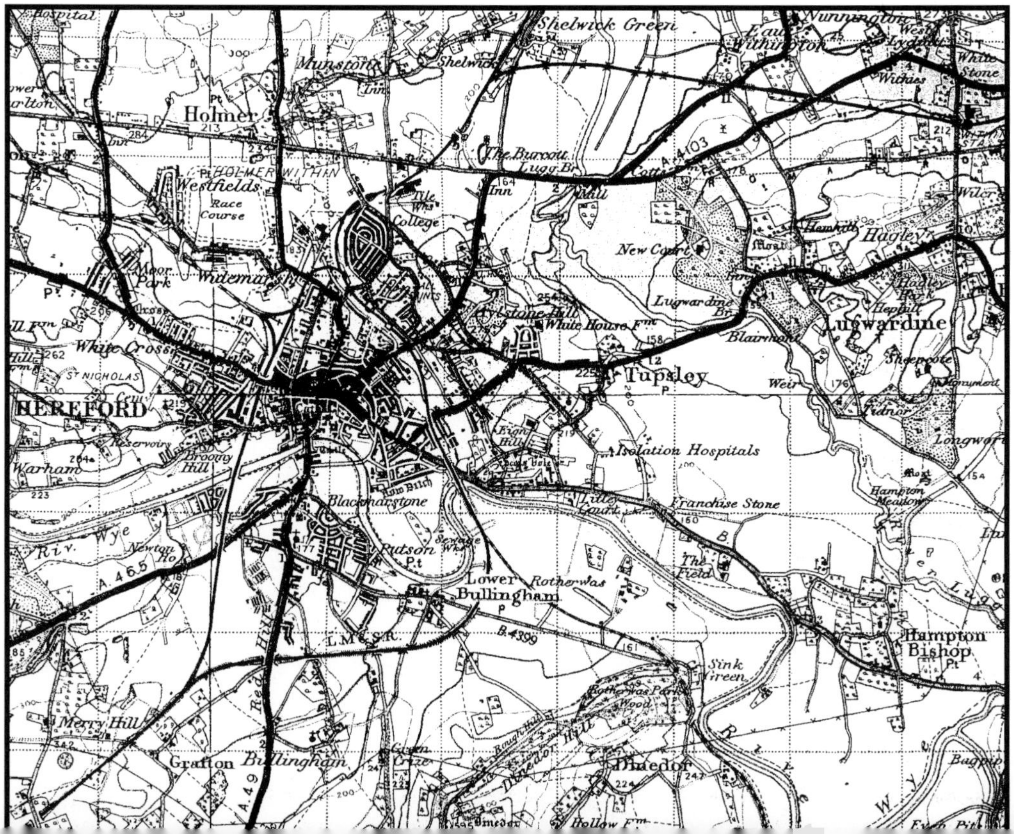

IV.   A closer look at the west side of the city in 1930 shows the then goods-only station at 6ins to 1 mile. Lower right is the route of the Hereford Railway, which terminated at a wharf. The curve was relaid as a standard gauge siding and was in use from about 1855; it had gone by 1888. Most of the MR trains from Swansea via Brecon terminated at Moorfields (near the southern apex of the triangular junction) from 1869 to 1874, but otherwise they ran to Barton until 1893. They were then diverted to Barrs Court, along with all trains from Newport. The Midland Railway engine shed within the triangle was in use from 1894 to 1924. The subsequent sole shed is shown close to the cider works. The large goods shed was opened by the MR in 1893. Bulmers Cider was actively involved in railway preservation from 1968 to 1993, using part of the area within the triangle, but this is outside the geographical coverage of this album.

2. This view was recorded as including MR 0-4-4T no. 1734 with a train arriving from Brecon and an LNWR 0-4-4T on the shuttle service to Barrs Court station. There were eight such trips each way on weekdays in 1877. Travellers had to suffer the inconvenience of two stations for 40 years. Note the wagon turntable in the foreground and that the signals are clustered around the signal box. (Kidderminster Railway Museum)

3. Barton signal box replaced three others in 1894 and was at the far end of the platform on the left of picture no. 2. It had 61 levers and was reduced to a ground frame when freight traffic southwards ceased on 31st

July 1966. On the left, a line curves to Watkins Bros. flour mill. The siding was in use from 1895 until 1975. On the extreme left is the banana warehouse, while the joint engine shed and coaling stage are on the right. (LGRP coll./NRM)

4. All locomotive activity was eventually centred at Barton, away from the gaze of passengers. As was standard GWR practice, the coal stage was surmounted by a massive water tank and loaded wagons were pushed up a steep incline to a doorway - right. Seen on 5th January 1958 is ex-LMS "Royal Scot" class 4-6-0 no. 46140 *The King's Royal Rifle Corps*. (H.C.Casserley)

5. Centre is the eight-road running shed and on the left are the repair shops in this 1962 view. Clear of wagons are the goods running lines which were at their busiest during World War I, when Welsh steam coal was required in vast quantities by the Navy in Scotland. (F.Hornby)

6. Water columns and ash pits were sited north of the shed and the turntable was beyond the right border of this photo of no. 7307, which was taken shortly before the shed closed on 2nd November 1964. (Nelson coll./T.Walsh)

HEREFORD - BARRS COURT

V. This map continues from no. IV and features the eastern part of the city, together with its sole passenger station after 1893. It was known as Barrs Court until that time. Top left is the former LNWR engine shed which was in use until 1938; the associated turntable lasted a further 20 years. The sidings south of the station served Hereford Corporation's oil depot.

7. This elegant structure was finished in 1884 and was the third on the site. The first was a temporary affair which was replaced in 1855. The west elevation is seen in about 1910. Records from 1923 show a passenger staff of 106 and goods 66; by 1938, the figures were 87 and 99. (G.M.Perkins coll./R.S.Carpenter)

8. We look south in the same era while an MR coach stands in the bay used by its Brecon and Swansea services. Until the 1880s, there was one through platform with two bays, the northern one of which could not accept broad gauge trains. There was a roof over the through track. (G.M.Perkins coll./R.S.Carpenter)

9. The south end is seen in about 1910. There had been a broad gauge engine shed near the right foreground until 1869. It later became a carriage shed. The bay on the left is seen more closely in the next photograph. (R.S.Carpenter coll.)

10. The once ubiquitous shunting horse was seldom photographed. Aptly it is about to move a horse box, which has its groom compartment nearest to us. At its far end is a section for fodder. (A.C.Mott coll.)

11. "Saint" class no. 2937 *Clevedon Court* is at the head of the 4.10pm departure for Cardiff on 8th May 1953. It would stop at almost all stations. The light engine is 2-6-0 no. 7308, one of the 4300 class. (T.J.Edgington)

12. Viewed from Commercial Road in the mid-1950s is no. 4952 *Peplow Hall* with an express for Cardiff. Empty stock is berthed on one of the through roads, while, in the foreground, are tanks (known as Cordons) which contained gas mainly used for dining car cookers. (A.W.V.Mace/ Milepost 92½ Library)

13. No. 5952 *Cogan Hall* was recorded shunting on 3rd June 1961. An engine had been allocated full time as station pilot to undertake local shunting exclusively until the 1950s. A large engine such as this was often "pilot" so as to be immediately available in case of failures. (G.Adams/M.J.Stretton coll.)

14. Seen on the same day is no. 6018 *King Henry VI* alongside Barrs Court Station signal box, which had 67 levers and was in use until 8th June 1973. In the background is the down goods shed and a staff footbridge.(G.Adams/M.J.Stretton coll.)

15. The crossover lasted until July 1966 and the down through line until July 1968. The latter was reinstated in June 1973. The two centre tracks were subsequently known as relief lines. (Stations UK)

16. The bridge carrying Commercial Road was at the southern end of the GWR/LNWR Joint Line, the track beyond it being GWR property. There was a carriage shed over the two unoccupied sidings until the 1950s. The signal box in this 1969 view was named Ayleston Hill until 8th June 1973, when it became "Hereford". (Stations UK)

17. A 1969 panorama includes both goods sheds; ex-GWR on the left and ex-LNWR on the right. The island canopy was subsequently greatly reduced in length. (Stations UK)

18. It is 19th May 1973 and we find footbridge repairs in progress following the canopy reduction. There was soon to be only one siding here, but a second one was laid in 1977. No. 1649 is southbound with ingot carriers. (T.Heavyside)

19. Moving on to 1st October 1976, we witness no. 47229 with assorted freight. The box remained in use into the 21st century having had its frame reduced from 69 to 60 levers in June 1973. A panel was added in November 1984, to control Shelwick Junction to the north of Hereford. (T.Heavyside)

20. Freight train frequency and length gradually increased. This is the 08.50 Mossend (Glasgow) to Severn Tunnel Junction service on 14th August 1984, during a crew change. The loco is no. 40044. (D.H.Mitchell)

21. Three for the price of one: no. 60097 brings in steel from South Wales on 26th March 2003 as a class 165 Thames Turbo waits on the left to leave for Paddington at 14.18 and a class 158 stands at platform 2, forming the 12.33 Chester to Cardiff. (V.Mitchell)

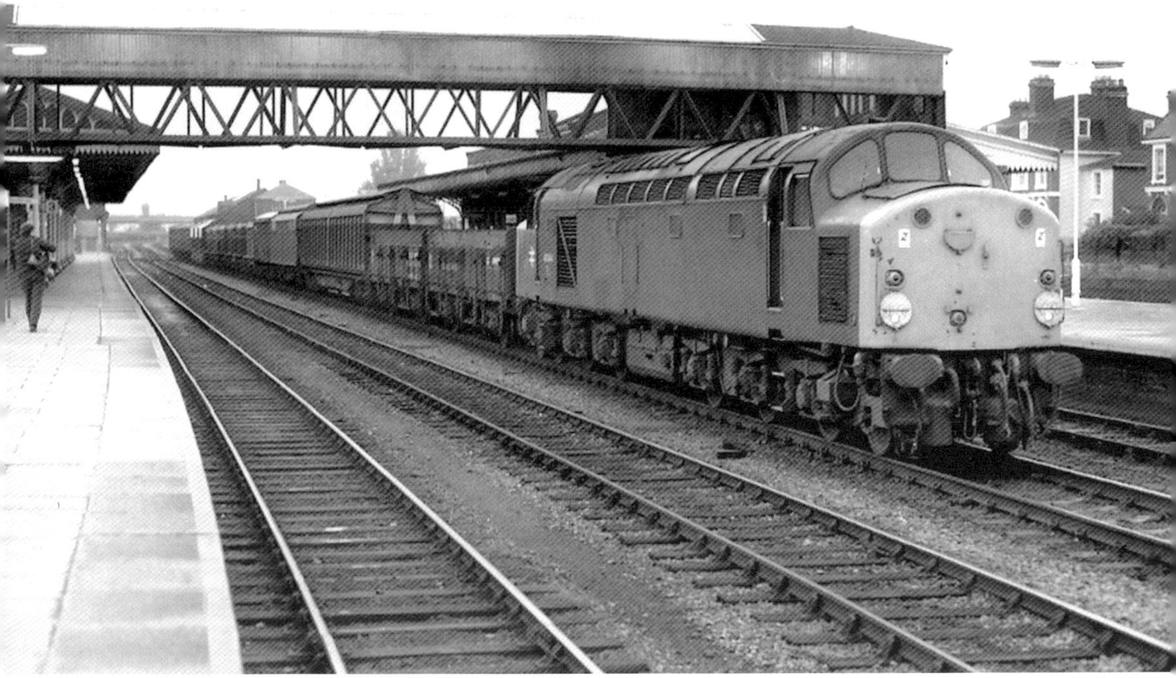

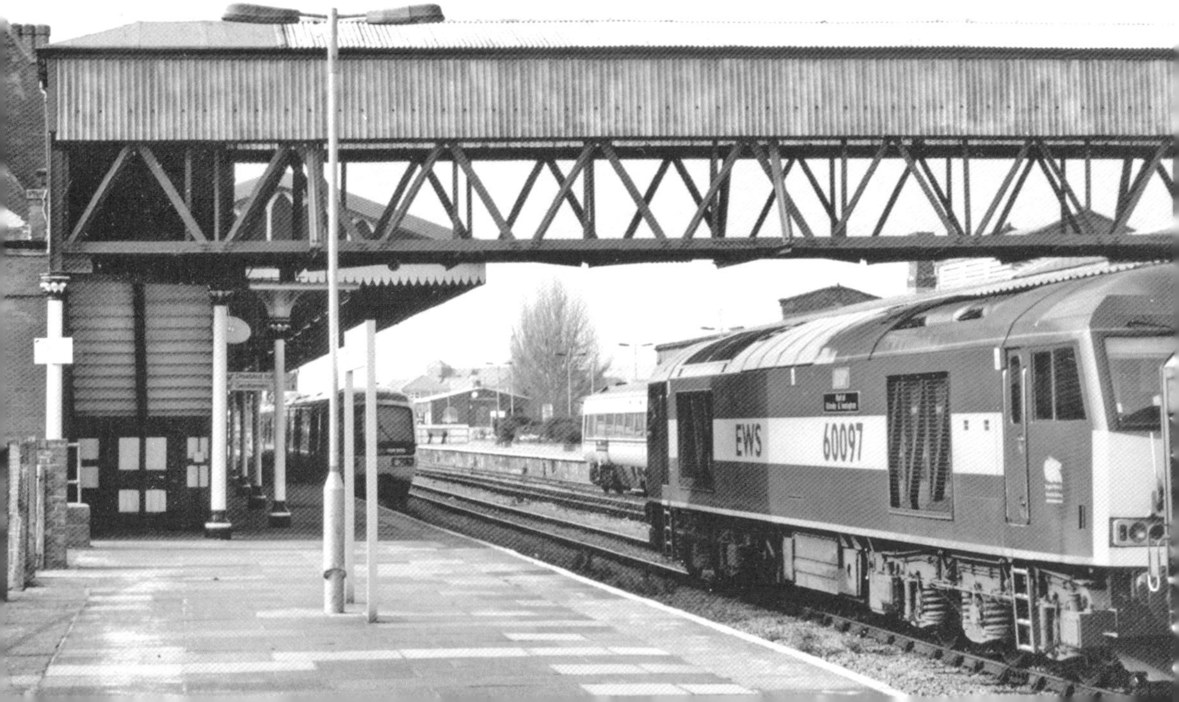
EWS
60097

SOUTH OF HEREFORD

← 22. A view south from Commercial Road bridge on 15th August 1984 includes Ayleston Hill or Edgar carriage sidings, one of which was extended to the oil depot of Hereford Corporation. It was also used for slaughterhouse traffic. No. 08932 hauls two tankers over the facing crossover, which had been changed from a trailing one in June 1973. DMUs have used these refuge sidings for reversal since their introduction and fuelling facilities were installed; hence the tank wagons. (D.H.Mitchell)

23. Rotherwas Junction was the point of divergence of the line to Gloucester. The route to Ross-on-Wye closed on 2nd November 1964, but the junction had been singled back in 1957. Part of the 55-lever signal box can be seen. It had 78 levers until 1925 and closed on 30th September 1966, along with the remaining sidings in the vicinity. No. D6901 is working an up ballast train on 4th March 1967. (M.A.N.Johnston)

24. Red Hill Junction was recorded on the same day, the 24-lever box having closed on 31st July 1966, along with the freight-only double track to Hereford Barton. The location is shown on map III, lower left. The 51yd Red Hill (or Haywood) Tunnel is about one mile to the south. (M.A.N.Johnston)

TRAM INN

VI. The inn was named after the Hereford Railway which ran along the strip of land to the west of it and its associated buildings. This 1929 map includes the down refuge siding (right track at the top), which was extended north to form a long goods loop for wartime traffic from 12th October 1941. There was (and is) little habitation nearby. The road is the B4348.

Tram Inn	1903	1913	1923	1933
Passenger tickets issued	7169	6212	5601	1445
Season tickets issued	*	*	38	19
Parcels forwarded	4978	5644	5250	5268
General goods forwarded (tons)	2292	2481	3776	1112
Coal and coke received (tons)	1052	781	2358	787
Other minerals received (tons)	2288	6932	5210	3204
General goods received (tons)	1305	1568	1829	424
Trucks of livestock handled	47	91	40	33

(* not available.)

25.   This northward view from about 1935 includes the main building in front of which was the up platform until around 1900. It was very short, being constrained by the goods shed and the level crossing. The staff dropped from 8 in 1929 to 4 in 1938. (Stations UK)

26.   We now have three pictures from April 1958. This one features the later up platform and its shelter. The next photo shows that the original one was very low. Passenger trains ceased to call here on 9th June 1958. (R.M.Casserley)

27. The Tram Inn is in the background as we examine the unusually extensive boarding of the track. Centre is a small wicket gate; its companion is close to the signal box, which had a special lever to lock them. Thus pedestrians could cross under supervision when the main gates were closed against them. (H.C.Casserley)

28. To the right of the camera was a crane of 2½ tons capacity. Goods traffic ceased on 5th October 1964. The photo includes the original up platform and a spare level crossing gate. (R.M.Casserley)

29. The cottage on the right was probably provided for the crossing keeper when the line opened. Passing over the crossing on 25th September 1963 is no. 48459, an ex-LMS class 8F 2-8-0. (M.A.N.Johnston)

30. The buffer stops of the goods shed road are evident as an express passes the rubbish strewn down platform on the same day. The locomotive is "Warship" class no. D860 *Victorious*. (M.A.N.Johnston)

31. The signal box had a 23-lever frame and was in use from 1894. Full lifting barriers came into use on 27th January 1974 and the box was still functioning in 2005, but the down goods loop lasted only to about 2000. (C.L.Caddy coll.)

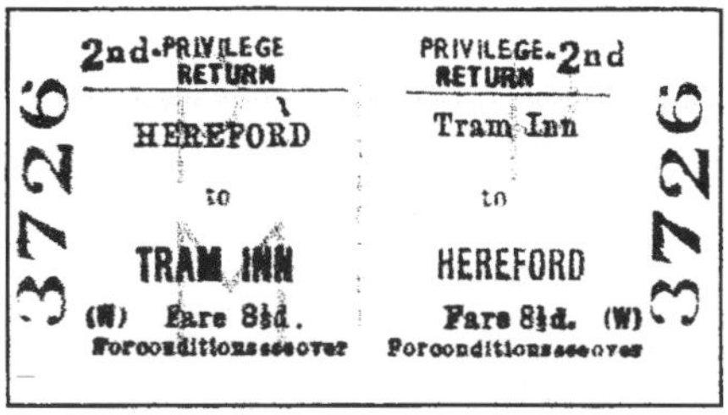

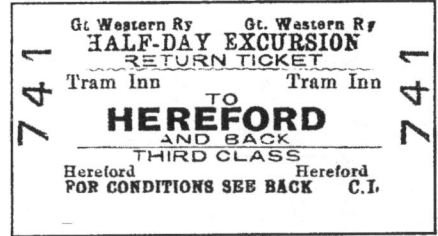

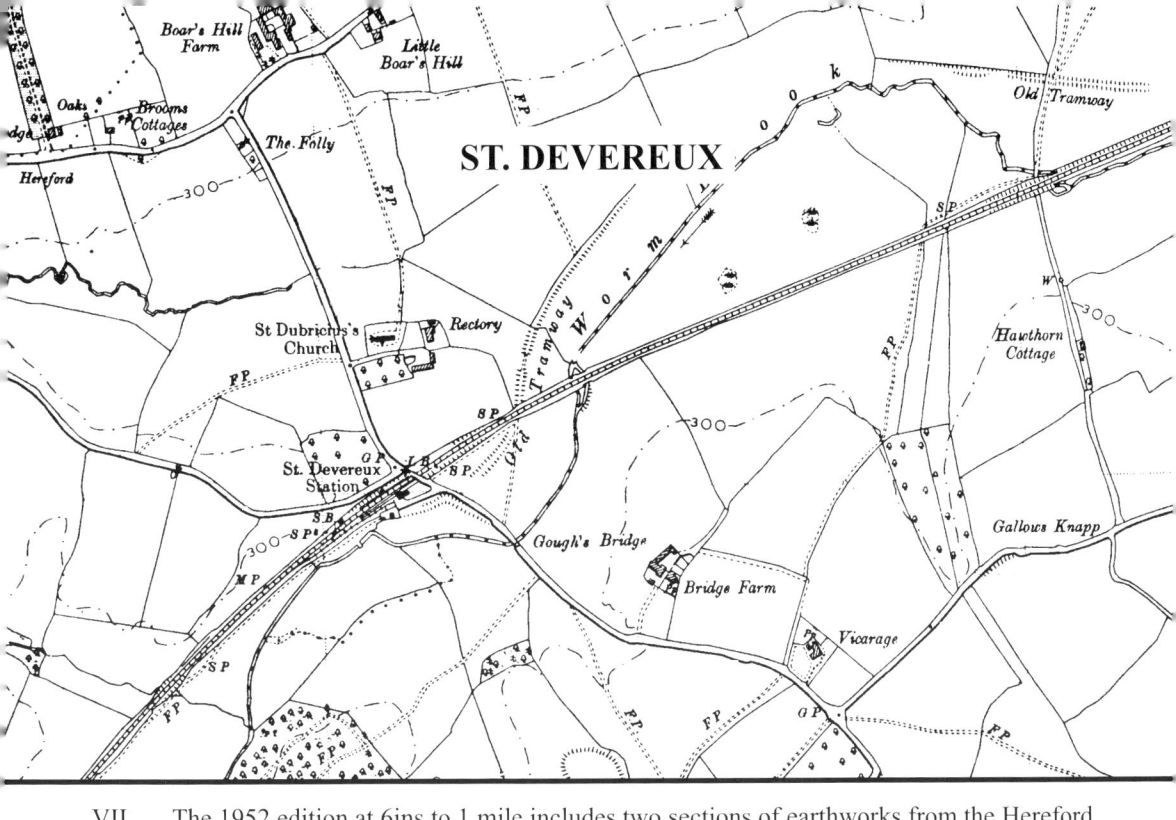

VII.   The 1952 edition at 6ins to 1 mile includes two sections of earthworks from the Hereford Railway. The present track is on the old alignment south of this station and also north of Tram Inn. This is another place with few local residents.

32.   Transfer of timber from road to rail is in progress in this 1935 photo; no crane was provided here for that purpose. The signal box had 15 levers and functioned from 1880 to 8th June 1958. There was a staff of three or four in the 1930s. (Stations UK)

33. The only way for passengers to cross the lines here was by means of the road bridge. No. 2829 is running down at 1 in 294 on 23rd April 1958 with mixed freight. (H.C.Casserley)

34. Seen on the same day, the goods yard changed little during the life of the station. Both freight and passenger services ceased on 5th June 1958. (R.M.Casserley)

35. The 1829 tramway alignment was close to the fence in the centre background. The steps on the right once provided access to the up plaltform. The photo is from May 1962. (Nelson coll./T.Walsh)

36. The architectural detail could still be admired on 4th April 1970 as a van train roared north. (E.Wilmshurst)

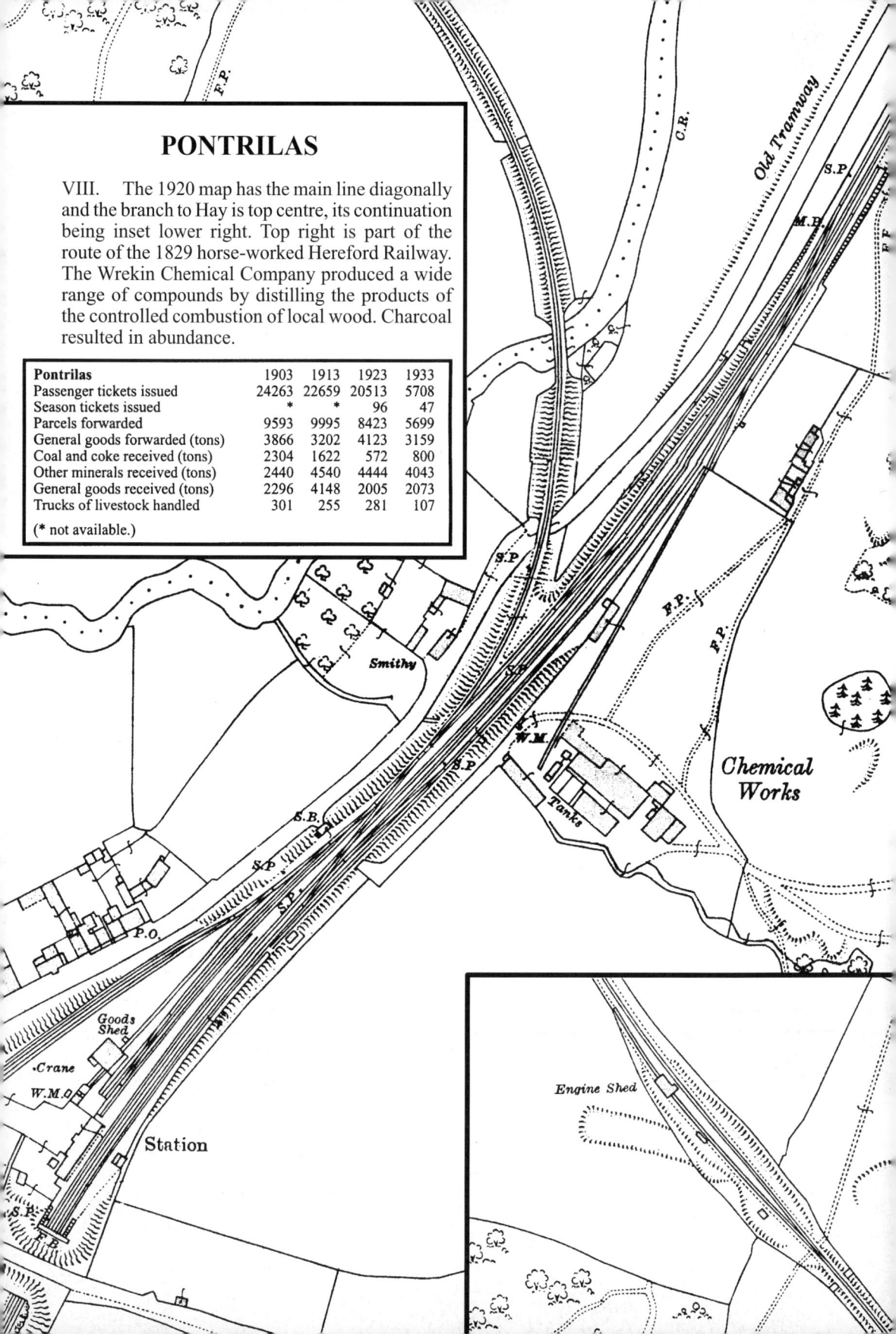

PONTRILAS

VIII. The 1920 map has the main line diagonally and the branch to Hay is top centre, its continuation being inset lower right. Top right is part of the route of the 1829 horse-worked Hereford Railway. The Wrekin Chemical Company produced a wide range of compounds by distilling the products of the controlled combustion of local wood. Charcoal resulted in abundance.

Pontrilas	1903	1913	1923	1933
Passenger tickets issued	24263	22659	20513	5708
Season tickets issued	*	*	96	47
Parcels forwarded	9593	9995	8423	5699
General goods forwarded (tons)	3866	3202	4123	3159
Coal and coke received (tons)	2304	1622	572	800
Other minerals received (tons)	2440	4540	4444	4043
General goods received (tons)	2296	4148	2005	2073
Trucks of livestock handled	301	255	281	107

(* not available.)

37. We start with three postcard views of this pleasant and attractive location. The 37yd long tunnel passes through a headland resulting from a substantial meander in the River Dove, which runs in the Golden Valley and joins the River Monnow half a mile south of the station. (R.S.Carpenter coll.)

38. A northward panorama from the footbridge seen in the previous picture includes a Golden Valley branch train in the bay platform. This line opened on 1st September 1881 as far as Dorstone, and passes over the bridge in the background. (R.S.Carpenter coll.)

39. This view includes another branch train, a small cart on the weighing machine (W.M. on the map) and timber lying close to the six-ton crane. There were 17 employees here in 1903 and still 15 in 1938. The main building was standing in 2005, in use as part of a garden centre. (Lens of Sutton coll.)

40. A down express rumbles over the connection to the branch and will soon be subjected to the pressure effects of the short tunnel. To the south was Llansilio box which had 11 levers and closed in 1915. The branch served a Ministry of Defence depot until 31st March 1969. (SLS coll.)

41. Comparison with the earlier pictures shows that the main building was extended southwards over the site of the water tank. On the right is the chimney of the chemical works, which had a private siding from 1874, until the end of 1929. (LGRP/NRM)

42. No. 6000 *King George V* runs south from its base at Bulmers' Hereford depot with the Severn Valley Railway's GWR liveried coaches on 3rd July 1977. It is approaching the site of the station, but the smoke near the second coach partially obscures the signal box. (T.Heavyside)

43. The 16.02 Crewe to Cardiff was recorded on 14th August 1984, along with the up and down loops. They had been created in 1941 by extending sidings. The down one was not used after May 1983 and was removed in 1989; the up one was still in use in 2005. (D.H.Mitchell)

44. The 12.12 Manchester to Cardiff "Sprinter" is seen from the signal box on 8th May 1989. The 42-lever box was still in use in 2005, but local passenger service had been withdrawn on 9th June 1958 and goods on 12th October 1964. The siding in the foreground was used for timber traffic from Scotland from 24th June 1997. (P.G.Barnes)

PANDY

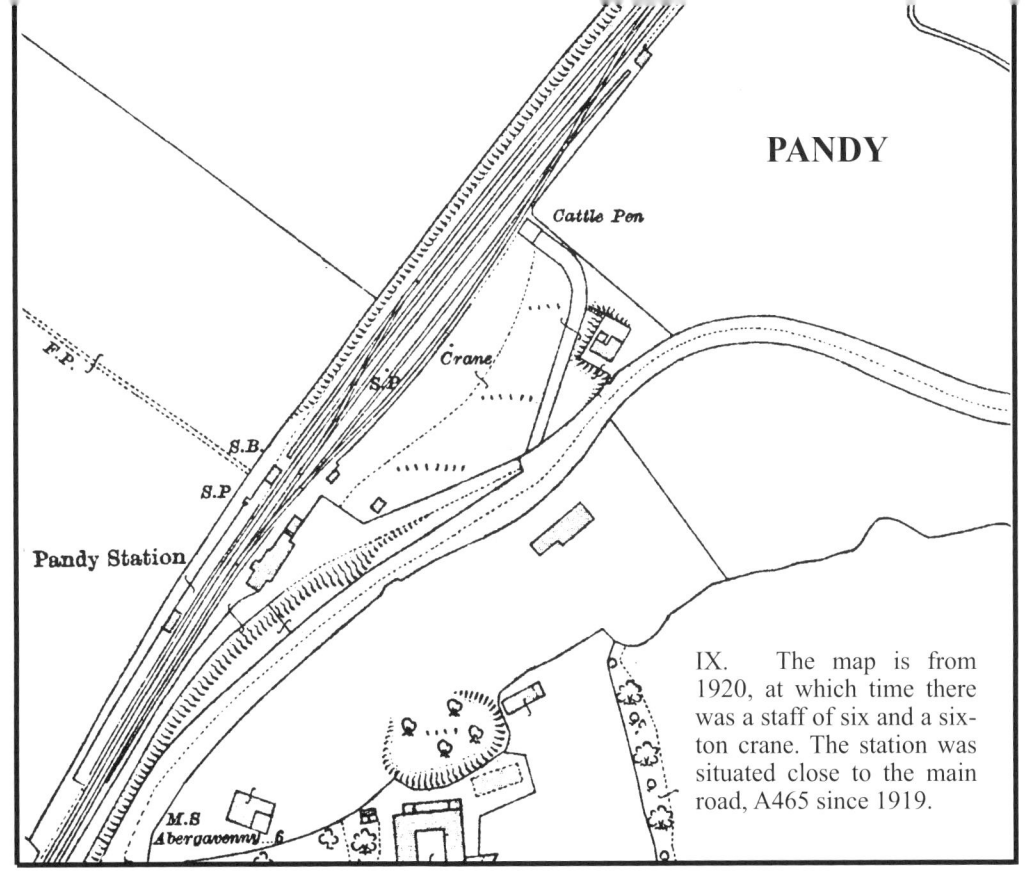

IX. The map is from 1920, at which time there was a staff of six and a six-ton crane. The station was situated close to the main road, A465 since 1919.

45. Approaching in May 1950 is no. 7017 *G.J.Churchward*, a "Castle" class 4-6-0. It is viewed from the centre of the next picture. The sign on the right indicates a long-forgotten service provided at some rural locations, for cash. (Nelson coll./T.Walsh)

46. Both passenger and goods facilities were withdrawn on 9th June 1958 and the west elevation was recorded in May 1964. The building was completed in about 1905 and replaced an 1880 structure which had been destroyed by fire. (P.J.Garland/R.S.Carpenter)

47. A bidirectional goods loop passed behind the signal box from August 1925 until January 1966. The box had a 30-lever frame and was in use until 3rd February 1982. This is a 1964 photo. (P.J.Garland/R.S.Carpenter)

SOUTH OF PANDY

48. There is a climb at about 1 in 100 for around three miles to the summit at Llanvihangel for southbound trains, such as this freight in May 1950. It is approaching a half-circle bend in the Afon Honddu, which it will cross as it leaves the valley. (Nelson coll./T.Walsh)

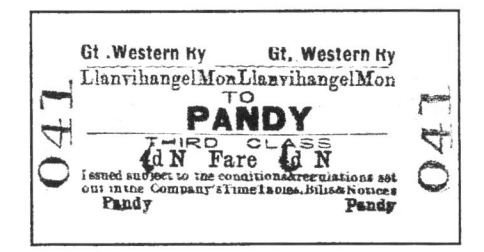

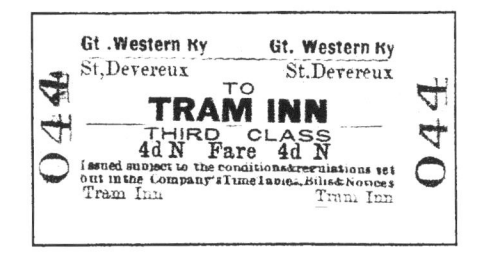

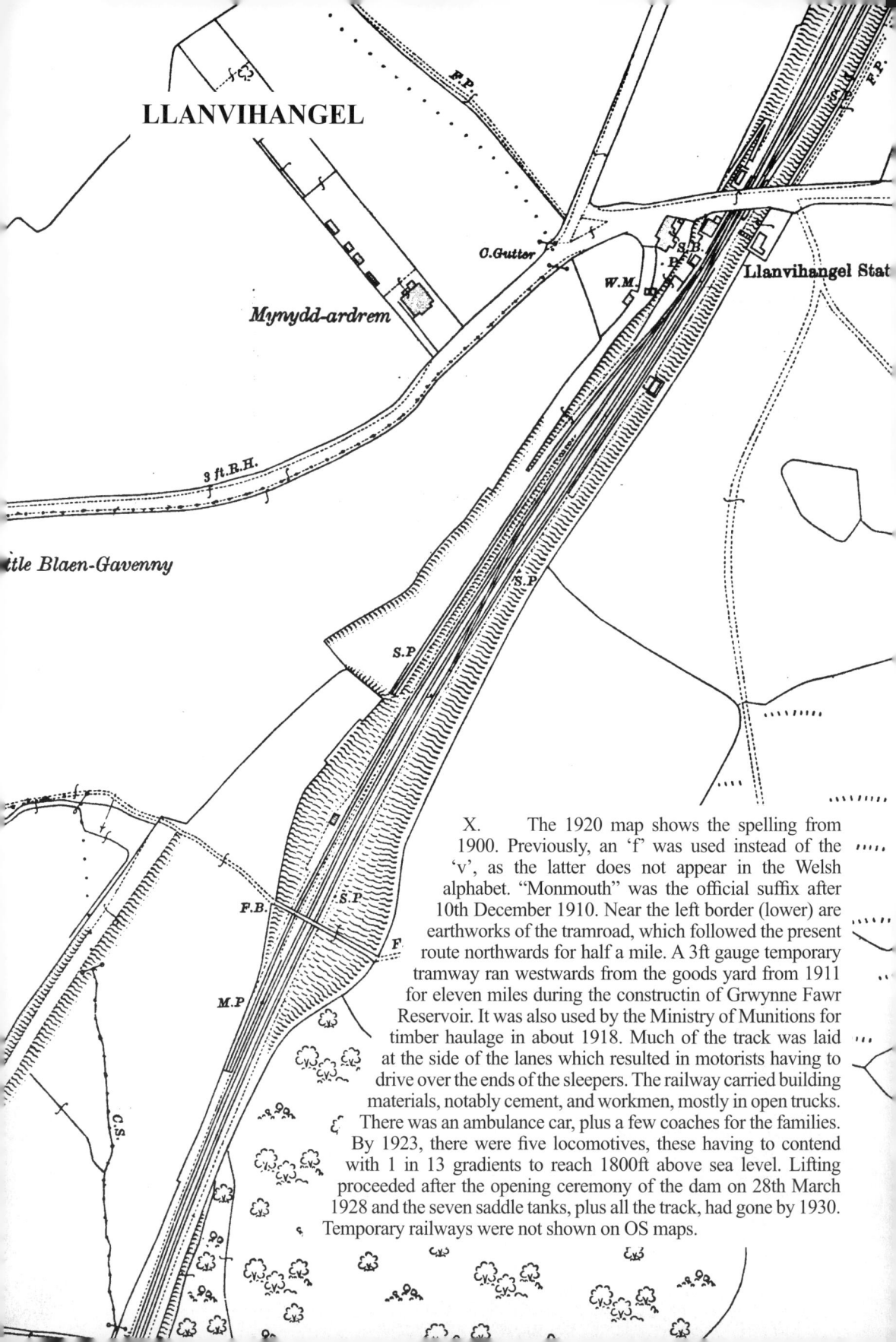

LLANVIHANGEL

Mynydd-ardrem

O.Gutter

W.M. S.B.

Llanvihangel Stat

3 ft.R.H.

tle Blaen-Gavenny

S.P.

S.P.

F.B. S.P.

F

M.P.

C.S.

X. The 1920 map shows the spelling from 1900. Previously, an 'f' was used instead of the 'v', as the latter does not appear in the Welsh alphabet. "Monmouth" was the official suffix after 10th December 1910. Near the left border (lower) are earthworks of the tramroad, which followed the present route northwards for half a mile. A 3ft gauge temporary tramway ran westwards from the goods yard from 1911 for eleven miles during the constructin of Grwynne Fawr Reservoir. It was also used by the Ministry of Munitions for timber haulage in about 1918. Much of the track was laid at the side of the lanes which resulted in motorists having to drive over the ends of the sleepers. The railway carried building materials, notably cement, and workmen, mostly in open trucks. There was an ambulance car, plus a few coaches for the families. By 1923, there were five locomotives, these having to contend with 1 in 13 gradients to reach 1800ft above sea level. Lifting proceeded after the opening ceremony of the dam on 28th March 1928 and the seven saddle tanks, plus all the track, had gone by 1930. Temporary railways were not shown on OS maps.

49. The platforms were staggered with most of the up one north of the lane to Crossways. The map shows a hairpin path down to it from the road. There was a staff of five or six here between the wars, to cover two shifts. (Lens of Sutton coll.)

50. The main line dropped steeply both sides of the station, this being evident on the south side in this view of the level sidings on 1st May 1962. No. 6820 *Kingstone Grange* has a good clear exhaust at the end of its full power exertion. Parallel to the train is the up goods loop, which lasted until 1964. (Nelson coll./T.Walsh)

51. A northward panorama on the same day includes the inclined roadway to the goods yard. Freight and passenger services had ceased on 9th June 1958. The sidings had been laid in 1873 and a down refuge siding appeared beyond the bridge in 1892. The main building is hidden by the trees, left of centre. (Nelson coll./T.Walsh)

52. Crossing to the down platform, we see the points of the down refuge siding, which was in use until 1964. Passengers leaving this platform used the foot crossing and then climbed up beside the white fence in the distance. The signal box had 21 levers and closed on 24th April 1967. Prior to 1892, the platform had been opposite the up one. (Nelson coll./T.Walsh)

Llanvihangel	1903	1913	1923	1933
Passenger tickets issued	6642	8866	16350	1756
Season tickets issued	*	*	2	-
Parcels forwarded	1897	2028	2442	3757
General goods forwarded (tons)	236	449	152	252
Coal and coke received (tons)	591	1287	2622	241
Other minerals received (tons)	869	2756	1730	1723
General goods received (tons)	116	3492	4080	105
Trucks of livestock handled	-	-	-	-

(* not available.)

53. No. 47220 ends its climb at 1 in 95 on 2nd July 1974, hauling the 08.45 Newquay to Manchester. The building in the foreground is included in the previous picture; it has subsequently been demolished. (T.Heavyside)

54. Various sites near the station are ideal for enjoying the visual and audible pleasures of steam locomotives working hard in both directions. No. 6000 *King George V* was a fairly frequent performer and is seen on 3rd July 1977 with SVR coaches forming a special from Shrewsbury to Newport. (T.Heavyside)

55. Crowds gathered on 24th April 1982 to witness class 9F 2-10-0 no. 92220 *Evening Star* working the "Welsh Marches Pullman" from Newport to Hereford. It was the last steam locomotive built by BR and is part of the National Collection. (T.Heavyside)

ABERGAVENNY JUNCTION

XI. The 1920 map has our route top left and the station below it. The line from the left of the triangle is to Merthyr and was opened as far as Brynmawr in 1862. The junction station was at the top of the triangle until 20th June 1870. The branch was operated by the LNWR and intially most of their trains started from Hereford. The lower part of the triangle has a single connection at its west end, but no direct connection to the main at the south end. It was convenient for engine turning. Lower in the right column is a complex of buildings for the County Lunatic Asylum; its private siding lasted from about 1884 until 1964.

56. The station was owned and staffed by the LNWR and later the LMS. No. 1202 was new when photographed at the bay with the 8.35pm to Merthyr on 2nd June 1947. (SLS coll.)

57. Only the signal box, most of the signals and the main lines were GWR property. No. 1014 *County of Glamorgan* is speeding towards the junction with a Penzance to Manchester express on 8th September 1952. The parallel track is one of the exchange sidings. (Millbrook House)

58. An action shot from the footbridge on 10th May 1954 includes no. 6946 *Heatherden Hall* heading the 8.55am Cardiff to Manchester and a "Grange" with a down freight. The timber appears secure, but during rough shunts, the entire load would rise out of the wagon vertically and descend back into it. (T.J.Edgington)

59. The LNWR was rather mean in its provision for passengers when compared with the GWR at similar junctions. This northward view shows that the platforms were of sub-standard height. (LGRP)

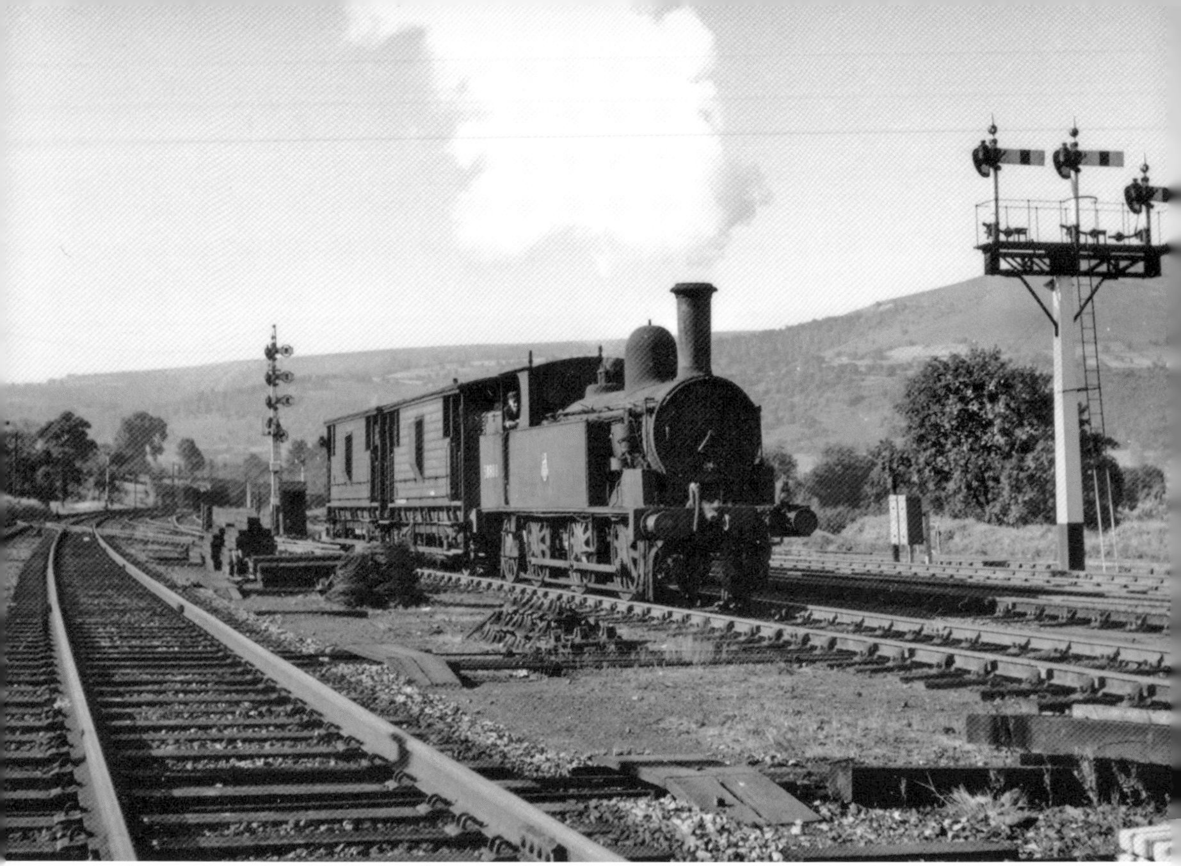

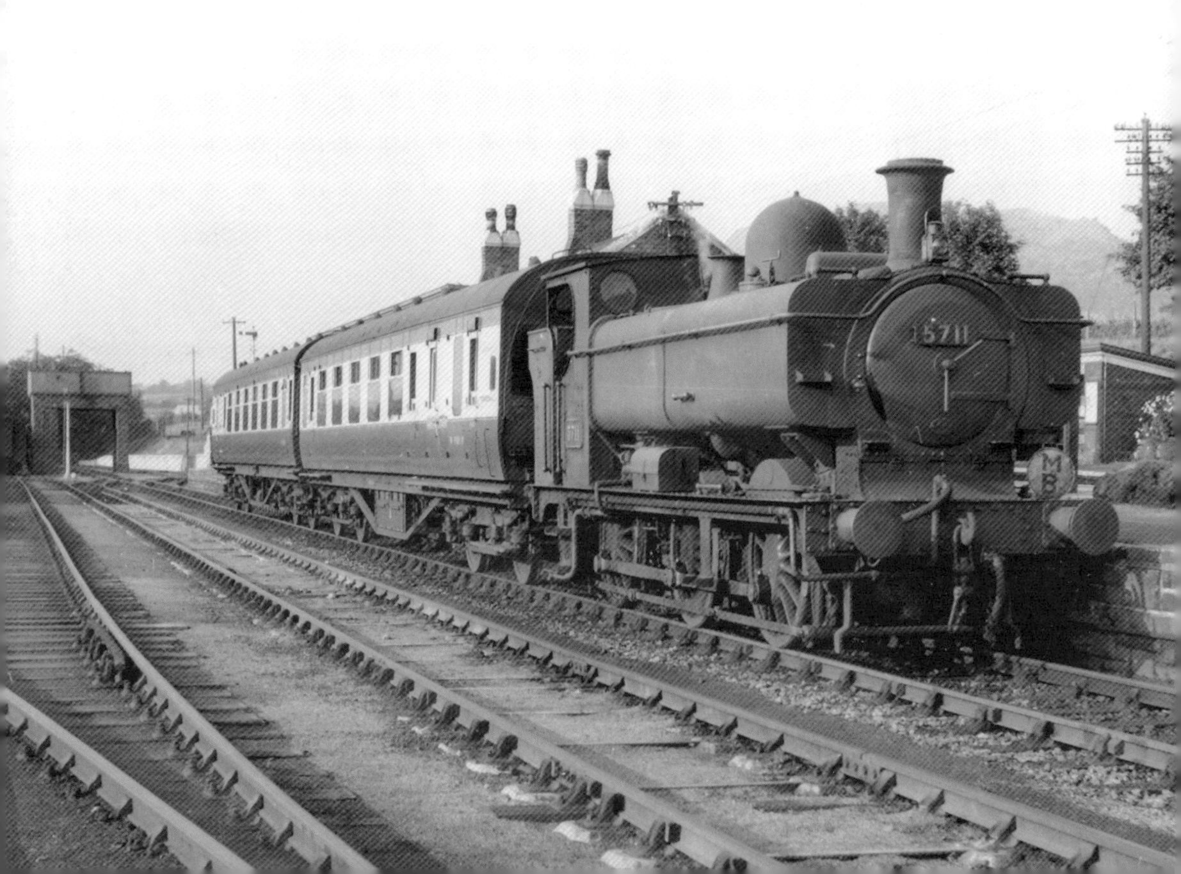

◄─────── 60. We look south along the up main line at South Sidings on 8th September 1952 as ex-LNWR 0-6-2T no. 58888 (once LMS no. 27602) responds to the lower signal in the background. The location is at the bottom of the left part of the map. The signals on the right are for trains from Brecon Road. (Millbrook House)

◄─────── 61. No. 5711 is in the bay on 16th July 1957 and is about to depart for Merthyr at 8.30pm. The route had been transferred from the London Midland Region to the Western at the end of 1948. There had once been a turntable beyond the water tank in the background.
(R.F.Roberts/SLS coll.)

62. An LMS signboard is evident on the left, while part of the 1920s carriage shed can be seen beyond the guns on the right. The signal box had 65 levers and closed on 14th November 1965. This southward view from the down platform is from July 1957.
(R.F.Roberts/SLS coll.)

Other views of this station and of Abergavenny Brecon Road can be found in
Abergavenny to Merthyr **(Middleton Press).**

63. The LNWR "Coal Tanks" were introduced in 1882 and were popular on the Merthyr route along the Heads of the Valleys. This line closed on 6th January 1958 and the loco is seen near the extensive carriage shed on the previous day prior to working the final train, an SLS special. The engine is preserved as LNWR no. 1054. (G.Adams/M.J.Stretton coll.)

64. The same loco is seen minutes later prior to being coupled onto the front of "Super D" 0-8-0 no. 49121. The station closed completely later that year, on 9th June. Part of the branch remained in use for freight until 5th April 1971. (A.E.Bennett)

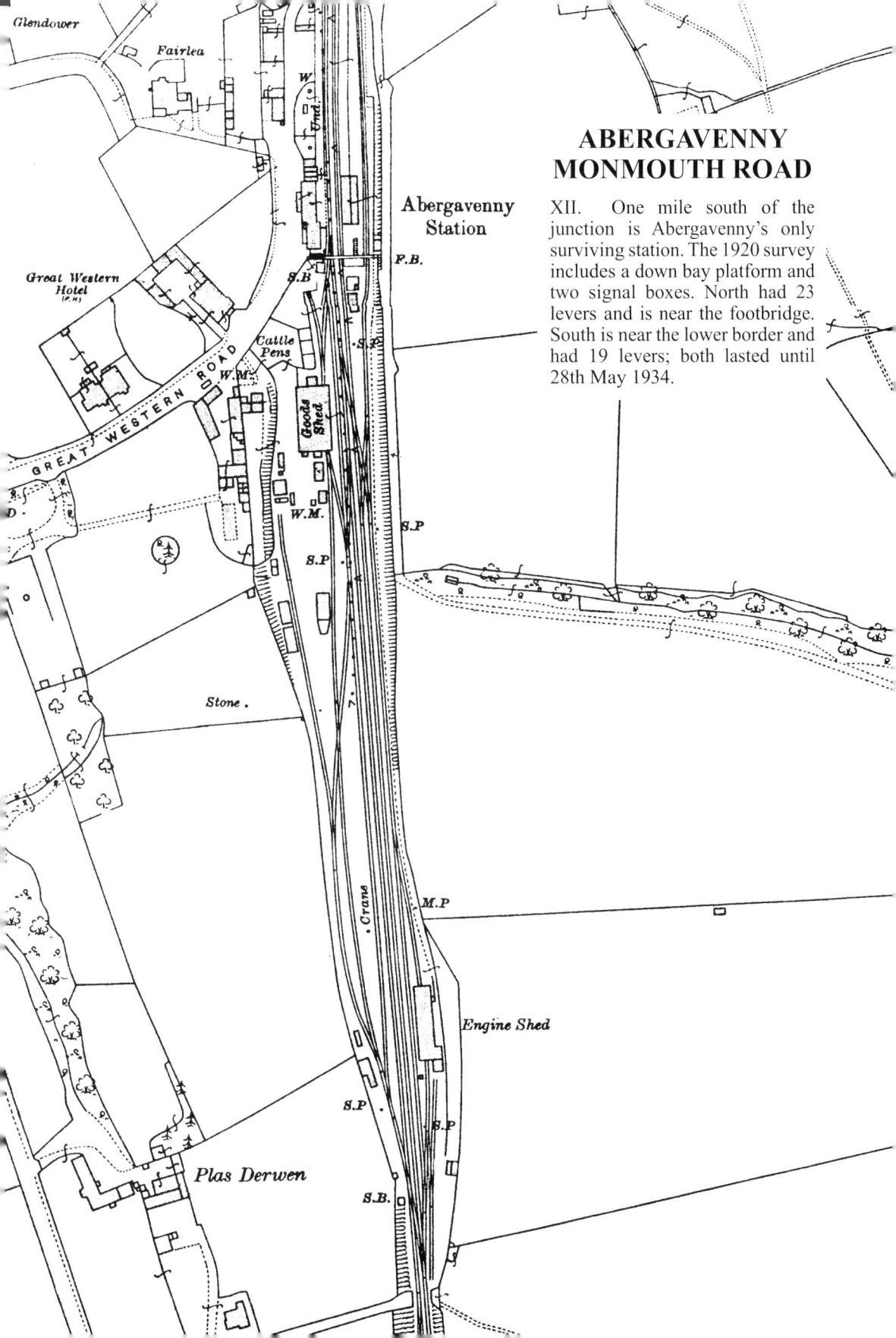

ABERGAVENNY MONMOUTH ROAD

XII. One mile south of the junction is Abergavenny's only surviving station. The 1920 survey includes a down bay platform and two signal boxes. North had 23 levers and is near the footbridge. South is near the lower border and had 19 levers; both lasted until 28th May 1934.

65. This indifferent postcard is included as it shows the entire original footbridge and that the bay platform was fenced off. There were 41 employees here in 1903, a busy place indeed. (G.M.Perkins coll./R.S.Carpenter)

66. The GWR were pioneers in road transport. One of their Milnes Daimler charabancs was used for a staff outing in 1908. The west elevation of the station is little changed today. (N.Lewis coll.)

67. A locomotive is blowing off at the goods shed door in this view from about 1962. The footbridge spans have been replaced; the left one has been seen earlier in picture 59. The suffix "Monmouth Road" was in use from 19th July 1950 until 6th May 1968. (Lens of Sutton coll.)

Abergavenny - Monmouth Road	1903	1913	1923	1933
Passenger tickets issued	70981	160289	69277	28519
Season tickets issued	*	*	221	157
Parcels forwarded	71492	75642	67892	53330
General goods forwarded (tons)	4347	4357	4726	3013
Coal and coke received (tons)	2620	2077	2403	2121
Other minerals received (tons)	3829	3481	5812	2560
General goods received (tons)	15066	16156	18764	13805
Trucks of livestock handled	719	990	1314	670

(* not available.)

68.　　A new signal box with a 52-lever frame was opened south of the station on 28th May 1934. It was still in use in 2005 and was photographed in 1973. (C.L.Caddy)

⟶ 69. The "Welsh Marches Express" called on 7th March 1981 and the photographer was able to record four of the five remaining sidings. Goods traffic had ceased on 1st April 1981. (T.Heavyside)

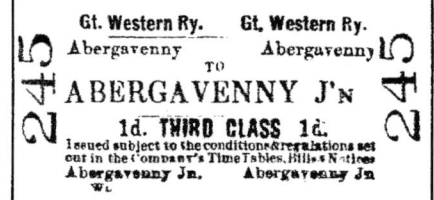

⟶ 70. We now offer a sequence of photos to cover the remaining sidings. From the early diesel era is no. D1674 *Samson*, with a train of car carriers, northbound. (R.E.Toop)

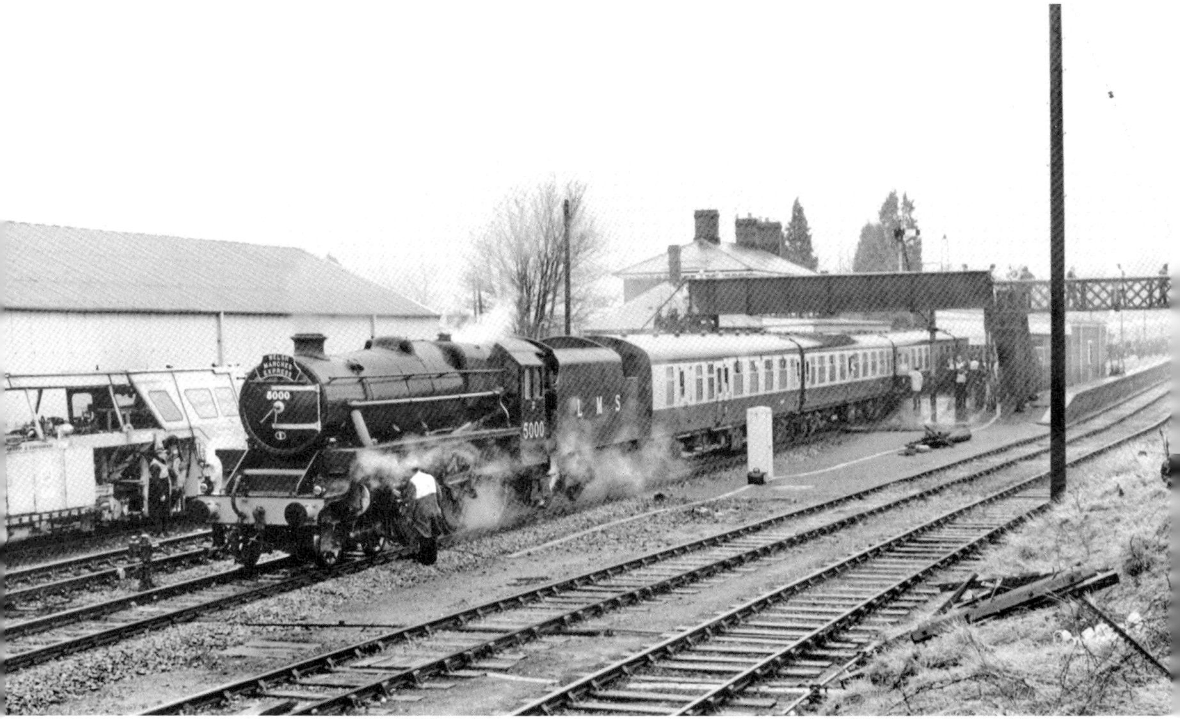
5000
L M S
5000

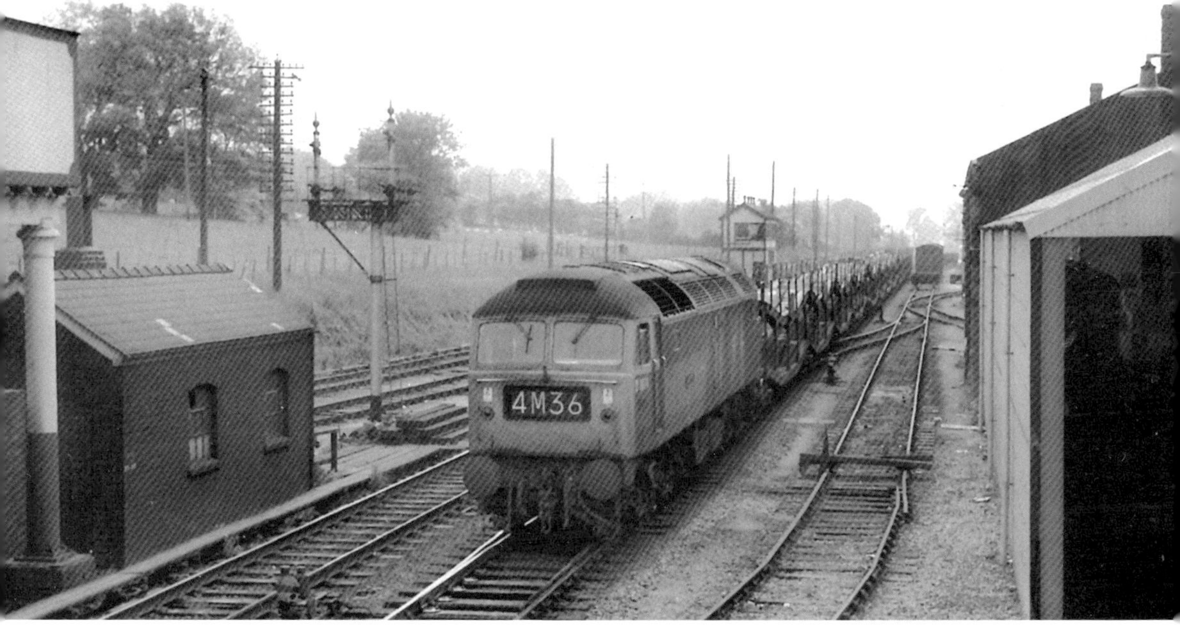
4M36

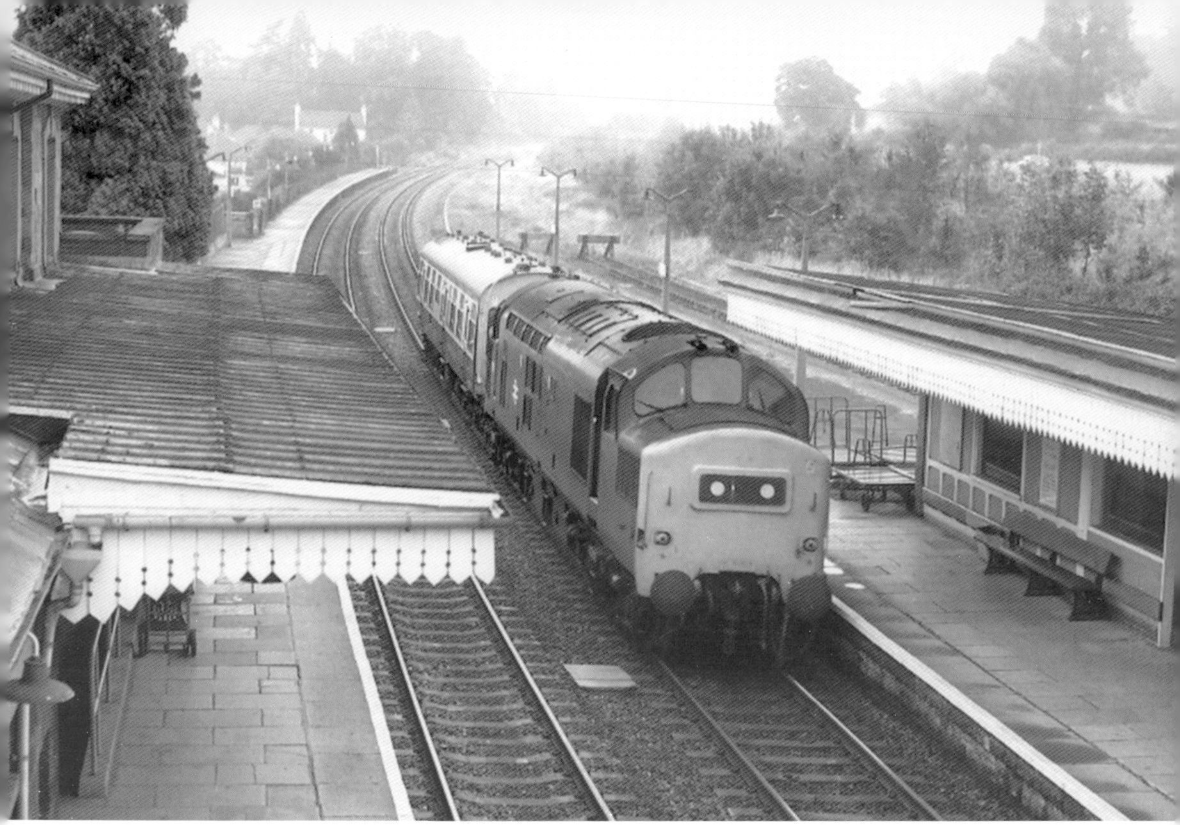

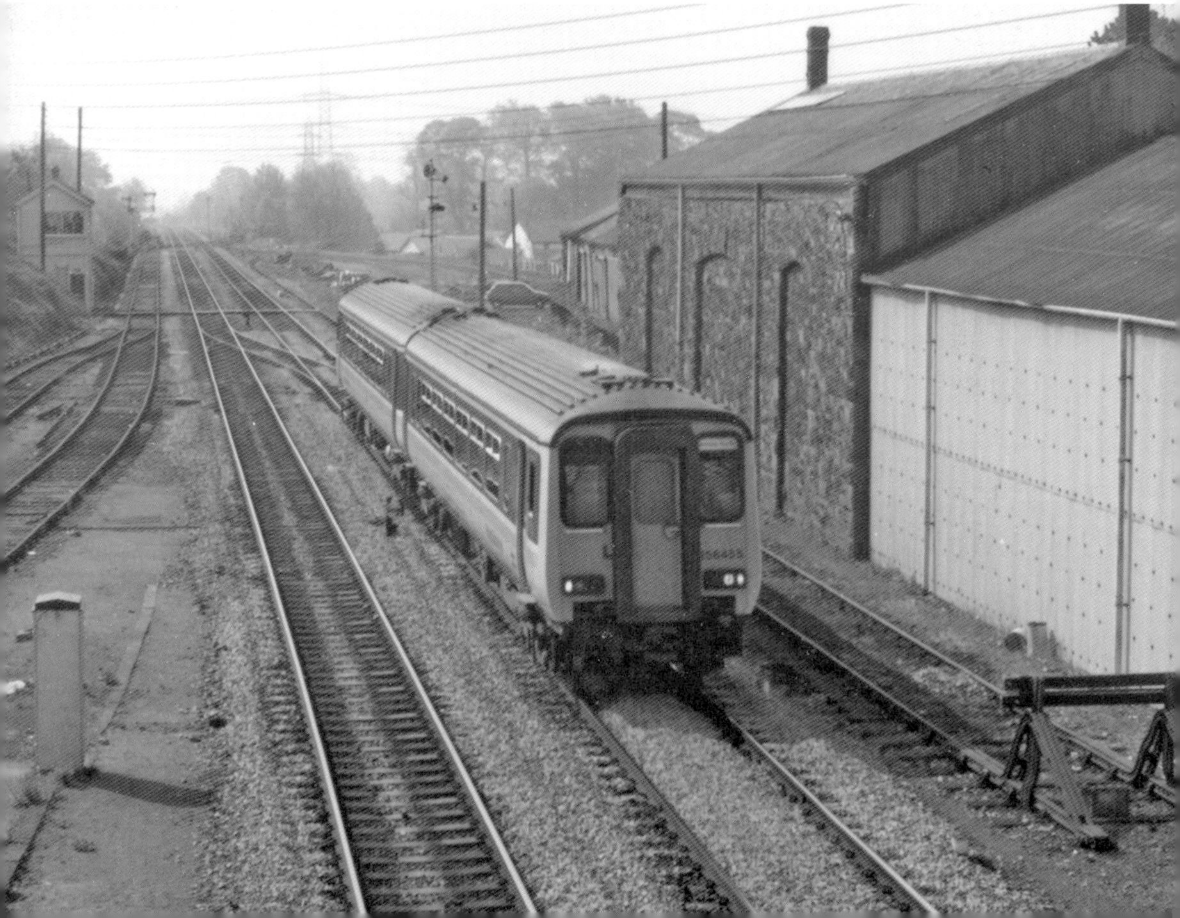

⬅——— 71. The buffers of the two eastern sidings are included in this shot of no. 37282 with an inspection saloon on 14th August 1984. These sidings had formed down goods loops from 1941 to 1967. (D.H.Mitchell)

⬅——— 72. This is the first of three photographs from 8th May 1989. It is from the footbridge and includes the former goods shed and "Sprinter" no. 156455 working the 10.02 from Cardiff to Manchester. (P.G.Barnes)

73. Seen from the signal box is the 11.05 Cardiff to Liverpool, worked by no. 156461. The up goods loop is in the background. (P.G.Barnes)

74. The same signals appear again as nos 37886 and 37711 roar south with hoppers. The station footbridge is in the background. The loop on the left was used for occasional timber traffic in the 1990s. (P.G.Barnes)

75. The DMUs had been upgraded by the time that the 12.00 Cardiff to Manchester service was recorded on 30th November 1991. No. 158771 departs, passing a GWR seat. (P.G.Barnes)

PENPERGWM

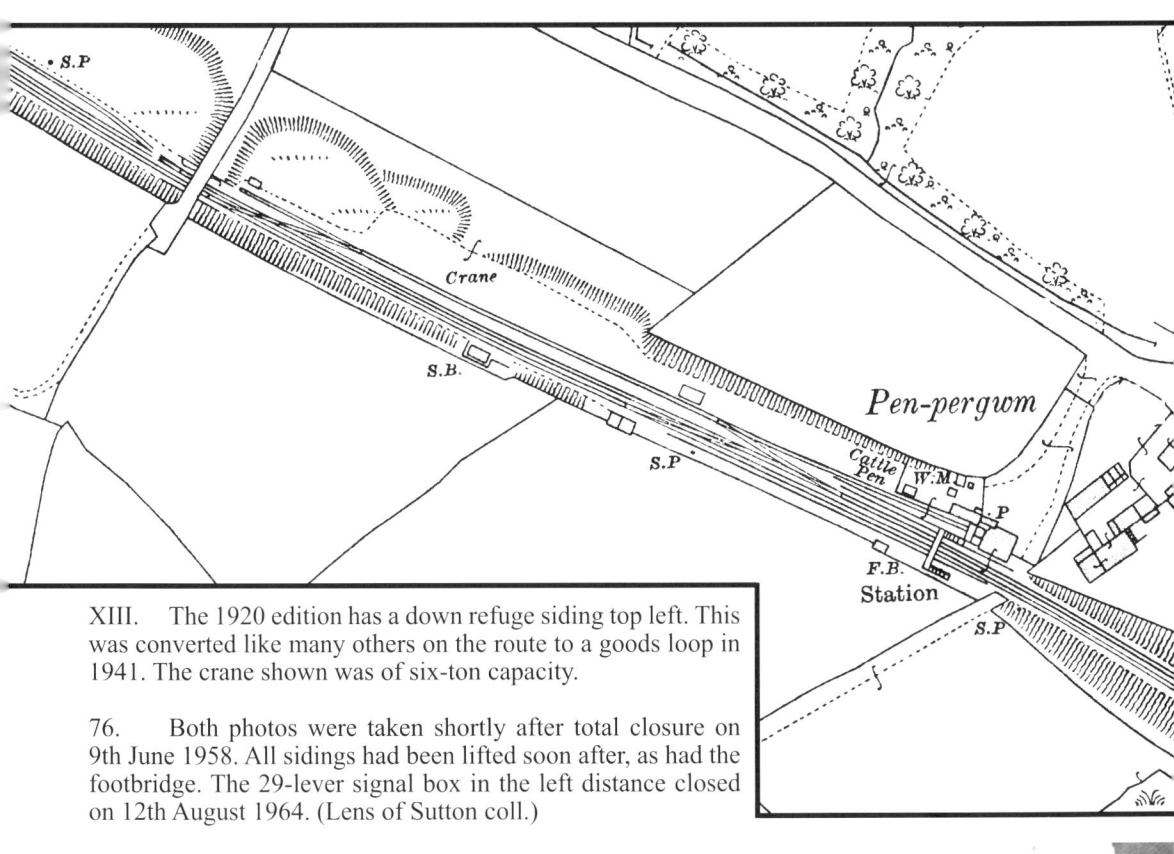

XIII. The 1920 edition has a down refuge siding top left. This was converted like many others on the route to a goods loop in 1941. The crane shown was of six-ton capacity.

76. Both photos were taken shortly after total closure on 9th June 1958. All sidings had been lifted soon after, as had the footbridge. The 29-lever signal box in the left distance closed on 12th August 1964. (Lens of Sutton coll.)

77. There were 5 or 6 men here in the inter-war period, but traffic diminished. This is the sad scene, post closure, looking towards Newport. The building survives as a residence. (Lens of Sutton coll.)

Penpergwm	1903	1913	1923	1933
Passenger tickets issued	16579	16793	16758	2909
Season tickets issued	*	*	56	19
Parcels forwarded	3198	3609	1672	1989
General goods forwarded (tons)	580	773	1665	619
Coal and coke received (tons)	1264	989	942	325
Other minerals received (tons)	1907	4843	1941	421
General goods received (tons)	631	1279	812	877
Trucks of livestock handled	26	31	68	17

(* not available.)

NANTYDERRY

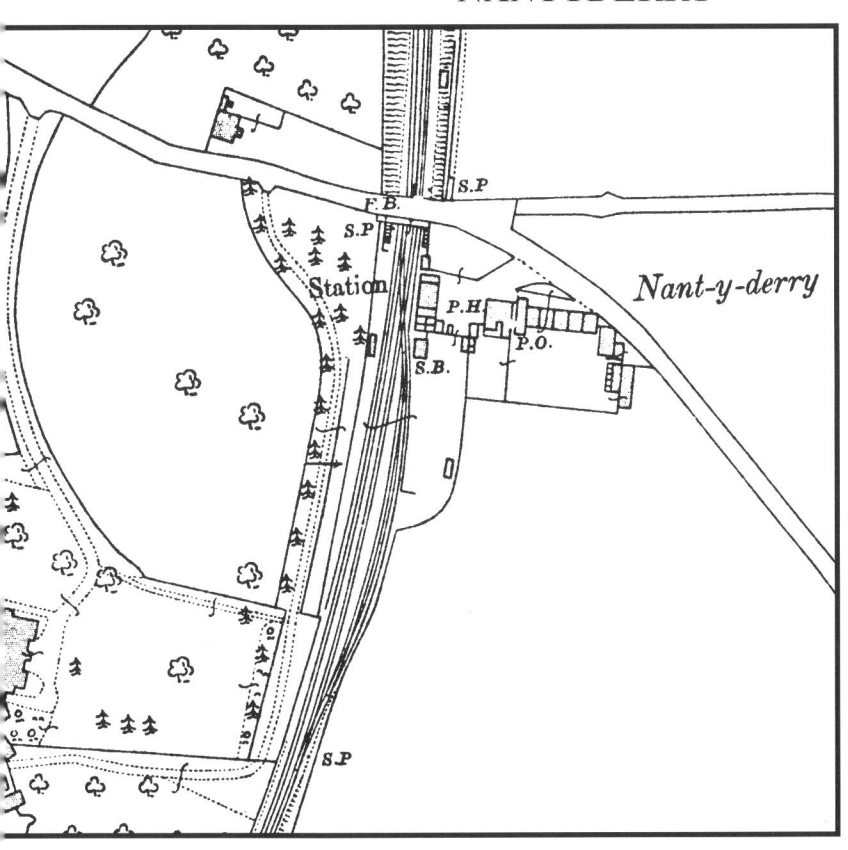

XIV. The goods yard comprised two short loops as shown on the 1920 survey.

78. The yard and station both closed on 9th June 1958, but the crossover remained until October 1965. There was a staff of six for most of the 1930s. (Stations UK)

79. The signal box had 26 levers and closed on 27th April 1980. The building was still standing in 2005, as was the station. There had been a station called Llanvair half a mile to the north until 1854. (Kidderminster Railway Museum)

Nantyderry	1903	1913	1923	1933
Passenger tickets issued	14225	16611	17387	3482
Season tickets issued	*	*	76	95
Parcels forwarded	2626	5228	5686	3591
General goods forwarded (tons)	488	711	608	210
Coal and coke received (tons)	1068	1215	1256	273
Other minerals received (tons)	1265	2178	1578	426
General goods received (tons)	963	1150	2931	695
Trucks of livestock handled	-	3	4	4

(* not available.)

LITTLE MILL JUNCTION

XV. The brickworks private siding passes through a gate near the bottom of this 1920 map. It was in use from at least 1880 to 1966.

→ 80. The station closed on 1st July 1861, but the platform on the branch was reopened on 1st May 1883. It is seen in 1952, three years before the passenger service to Monmouth was withdrawn. (LGRP)

81. A view towards the junction in April 1955 includes the 1925 signal box. The four exchange sidings seen on the map were increased to seven for wartime traffic and all but one were removed in 1964. The latter lasted until 1979. (R.M.Casserley)

82. Two miles of the branch to Glascoed were retained for military traffic and one such train was recorded on 8th May 1989, waiting for a southbound "Sprinter" to pass. The 55 levers in the box were reduced to 17 when a panel was added in September 1979. The branch was overgrown in 2005, having been taken out of use on 31st January 1993, but a small part was restored for engineering stock. (P.G.Barnes)

PONTYPOOL ROAD
Turnpike Cottage
Coed Cae Breast
Foundry
Pontymoile
PONTYMOILE
Panteg Cemetery
Mort. Chap.
Coed-y-canddo
Filter Bed
Pontypool Road Station
Coed y Canddo
Great Western Terrace
Maesderwen
Aqueduct
Weir
Lower Mill
Admiralty Siding
Station South Junction
Lower Mills Sheet Wks.
Canal Junc.
Pontymoile House
Galvanising Wks.
Vicar's Cottages
Monmouthshire
Towing Path
West Junction
Cae Pea Brake
Scrap Depot
The Elms
Allotment Gardens
Pres-coch
Old Quarries
Folly Reservoir (Pontypool Gas & Water Co.)
G.W.R. Eastern Valleys Line
Afon-Lwyd
Middle Junction
East Junction
Pont-y-felin Brake
New Park
Black Plantation
Schools
Melodia
Infirmary
Isolation Hospl.
Union Workhouse
Goods Shed
Sunnybank
Allotment Gardens
Sewage Tank (Panteg U.D.C.)
Pont-y-felin Wood
Pont-y-felin Road
Sun. Sch.
Recreation Ground
Springs
Griffithstown
Mary Street
Edward St.
Charles St.
Windsor Road
Commercial Street
Kemys Street
The Greenway
Panteg Foundry
Cricket Ground
Station
Pont-y-felin
Ford
Spring
GRIFFITHSTOWN
Drill Hall
Allotment Gardens
Hereford G.W.R. & Newport
Butcher's Wood
Curdy Farm
Panteg House
Ivy Lodge
Goods Shed
Panteg Steel Works
Reservoir
Greenfield Road
Panteg Hotel (P.H.)
Greenhill House
Panteg Sheet & Galvanizing Works
Pontrhydyrun Wood
Kemys-fawr
School
Panteg Junction
P A N T E G

XVI. The station is top right on this 1918 map at 6ins to 1 mile. The first had been on the other side of the road bridge until 1st March 1909 and was named Pontypool Newport Road until May 1854. It became Pontypool & New Inn in 1994. The next station south on the Hereford & Newport line had been sited near the latter word at the bottom of the map. It was called Panteg, but closed in 1880. There is a station nearby, on the adjacent route, called Panteg & Griffithstown. The lower line top left is for Blaenavon and closed in 1962. The upper one carried passenger trains to Neath until 15th June 1964. Below centre is a flyover and Panteg & Coedygric signal box, which replaced Coedygric Junction (2nd box) of 47 levers, opened late 1904, and both Panteg & Griffithstown North (2nd box) of 50 levers, opened in 1917, and Panteg & Griffithstown South (opened July 1880) with 15 levers. The new Panteg & Coedygric box opened 15th January 1937 and closed on 11th February 1980; it originally had 106 levers. In its declining years the frame was shortened to 17 levers. Panteg Steel Works (lower) had a signal box from at least 1901, but was latterly a 15-lever ground frame. Near the lower border is Panteg Junction; the 36-lever box was in use until 7th November 1966. There were still up and down goods loops in this vicinity in 2005. Branching from the former were sidings to Panteg Steelworks and from the latter to Pilkington Bros. (Fibreglass) Ltd. These were controlled by Little Mill Junction signal box, more than four miles north.

83. The pre-1909 station and its island platform is seen in this view towards Hereford, but its down bay platform is beyond the right border. (G.M.Perkins coll./ R.S.Carpenter)

84. The replacement station was a very spacious affair, with two through platforms and a bay at each end. This northward panorama is from the road bridge in the background of the previous picture and dates from the time of completion in 1909. (Lens of Sutton coll.)

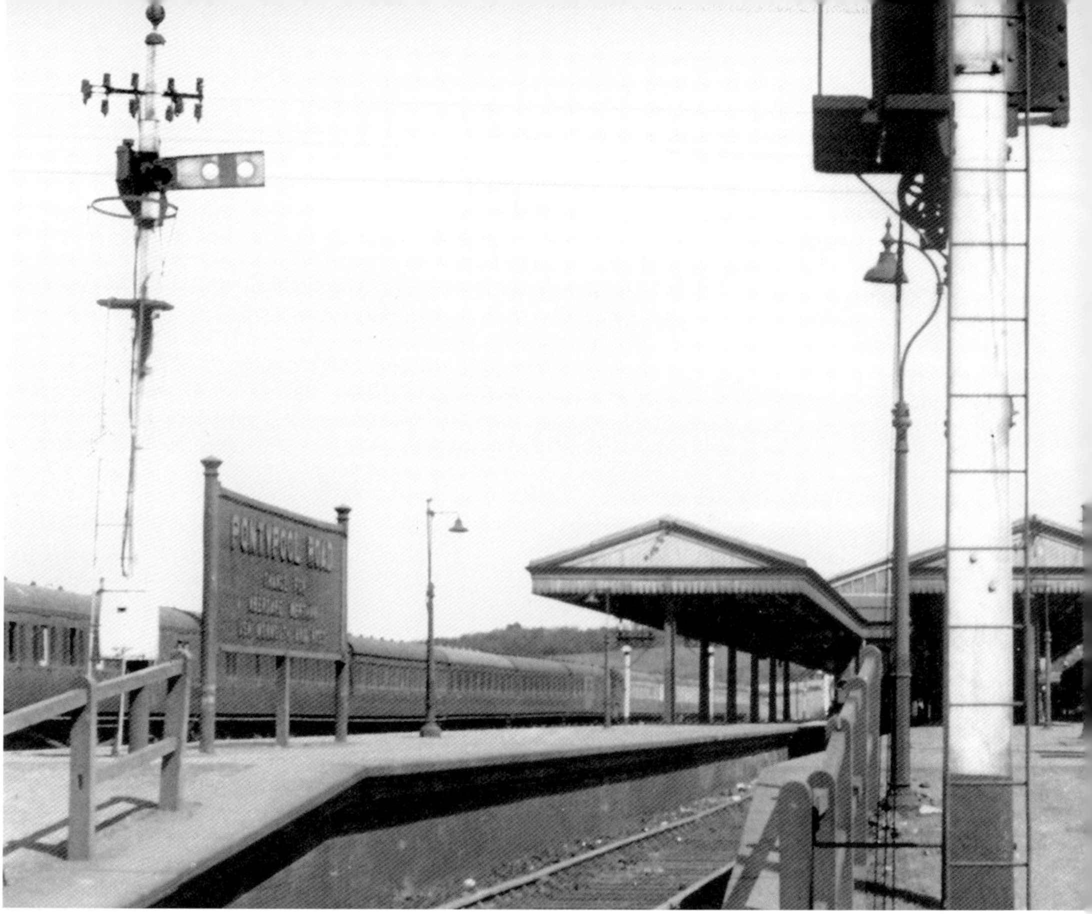
PONTYPOOL ROAD

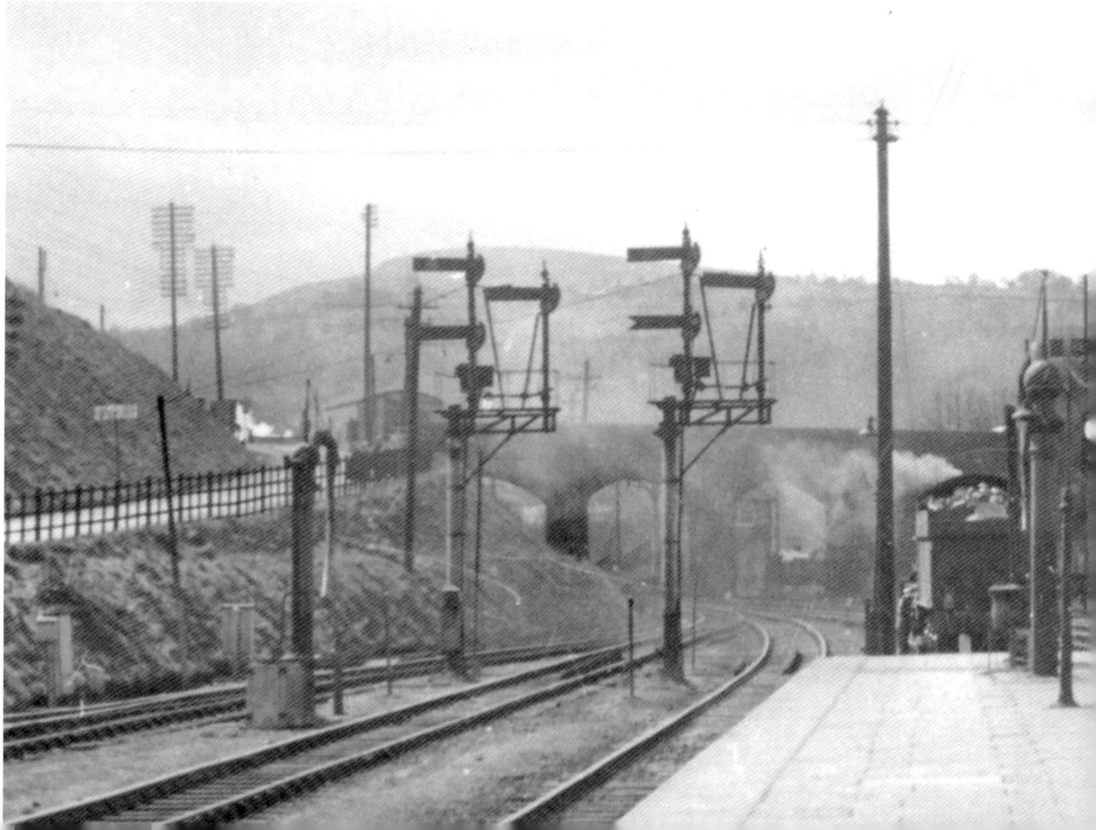

85.   Two photos from 1955 extend our survey of this impressive location. This is the southern bay, with a perforated shunt signal on the left. The one in the centre carries a route indicator box. (H.C.Casserley)

86.   A view towards Newport includes the approach road and an engine in the short siding between the platform roads. (H.C.Casserley)

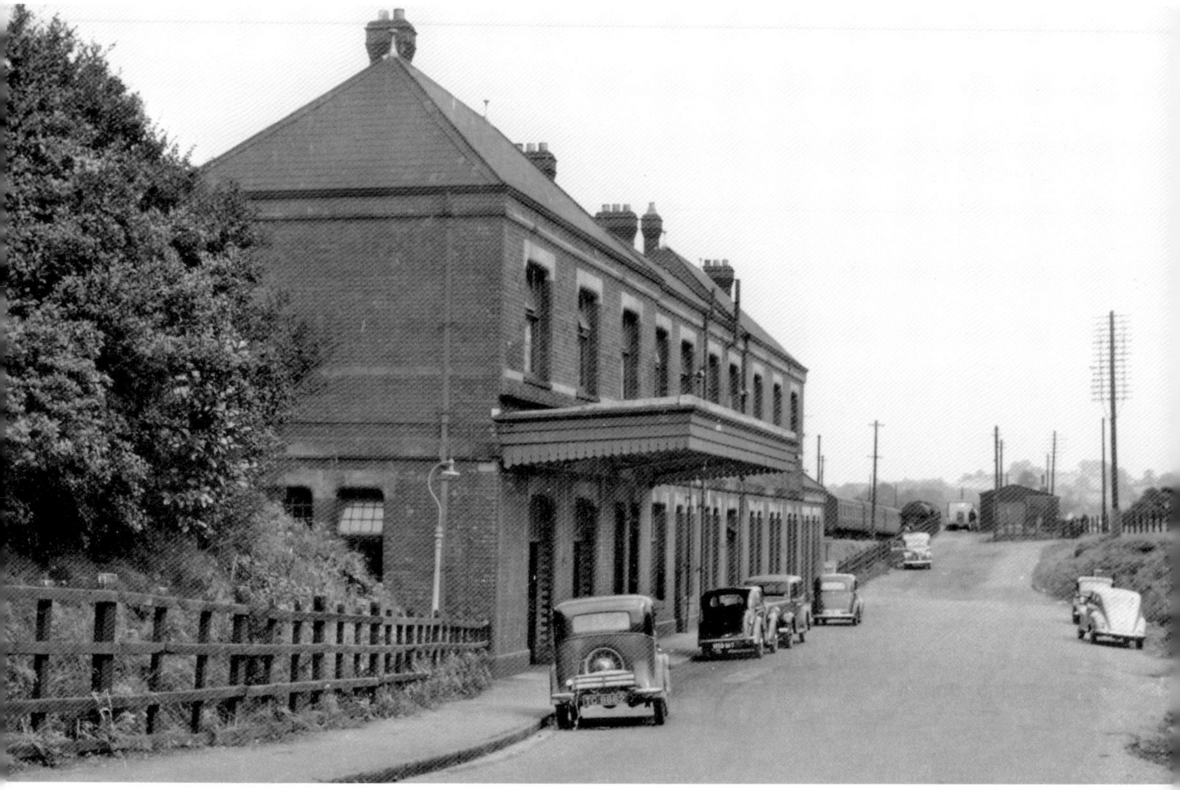

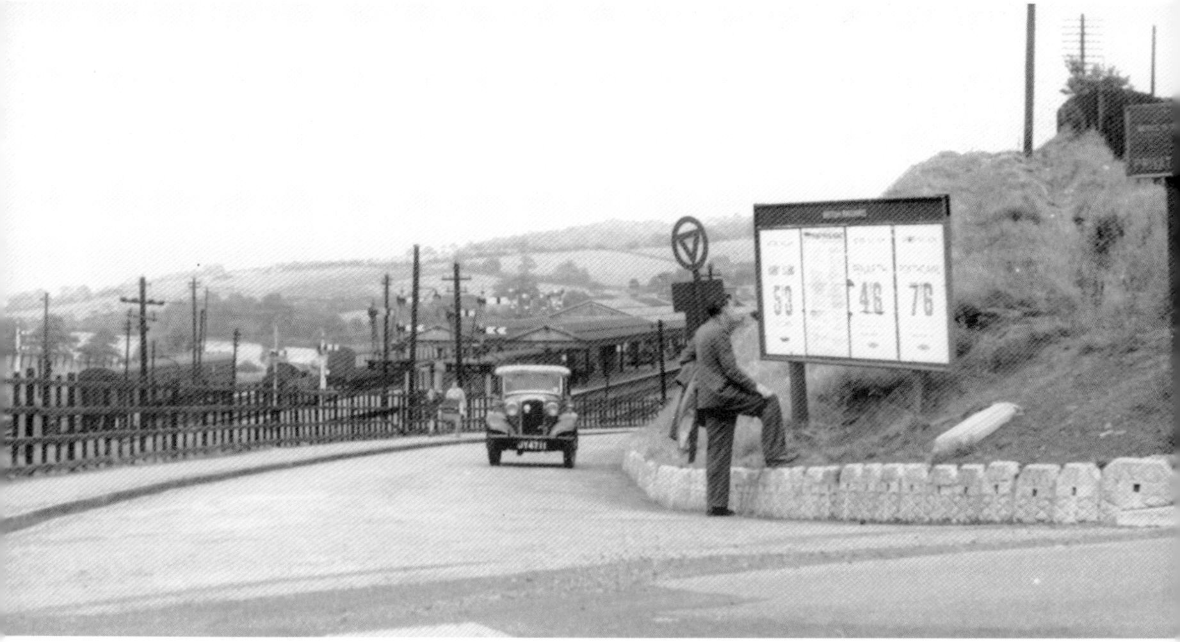
53
46
76

← ———— 87. The entrance building is on the right of picture no. 84 and is seen here in 1953. There were 77 employees here in 1923, with a further 38 involved in goods traffic. (Lens of Sutton coll.)

← ———— 88. A 1958 photo from the main road features the station approach with a contemporary HALT sign and a 1934 Hillman Minx. Trips on offer were for 5/3d to Barry Island, 4/6d to Penarth and 7/6d to Porthcawl. (H.C.Casserley)

89. Perfectly illuminated in the south bay on 4th October 1958 is 0-6-0PT no. 6431, probably bound for Neath. (G.Adams/M.J.Stretton coll.)

90. Running in with the 11.45am Manchester to Plymouth on 11th July 1959 is no. 6903 *Belmont Hall*. The down main line is to the right of it, the other tracks being carriage sidings. There were crossovers near the middle of both through platforms until 1967. They were worked from Pontypool Station Middle Box. Its two separate 13-lever frames became ground frames on 8th October 1957. (H.C.Casserley)

⟶ 91. A freight service is departing from the up main line on 5th May 1962. To the left of it were up and down goods lines. In the distance is Pontypool Station North box, which had 65 levers and closed on 4th November 1973. (Nelson coll./T.Walsh)

⟶ 92. The goods running lines are adjacent to the siding on the left in this northward view from July 1963. During construction, over 79,000 cu.yds. of material was excavated and a further 24,000 brought in from elsewhere to create a level site. Staffing ceased full time on 5th July 1971. (C.L.Caddy)

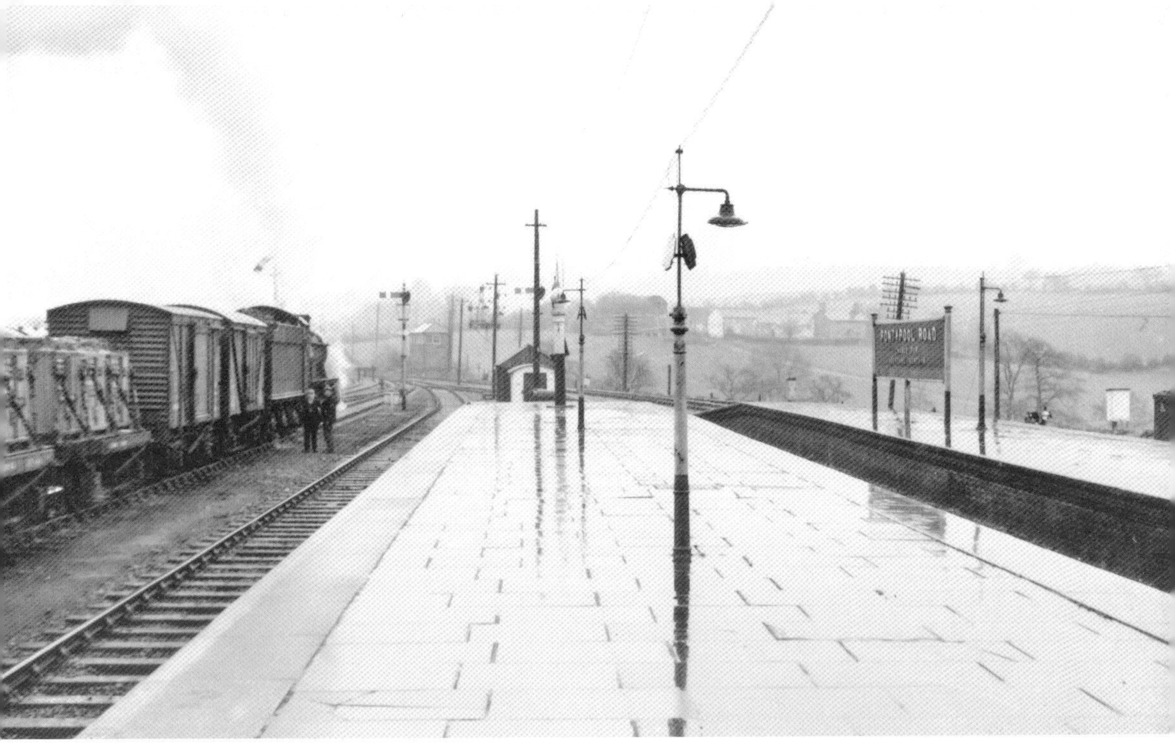

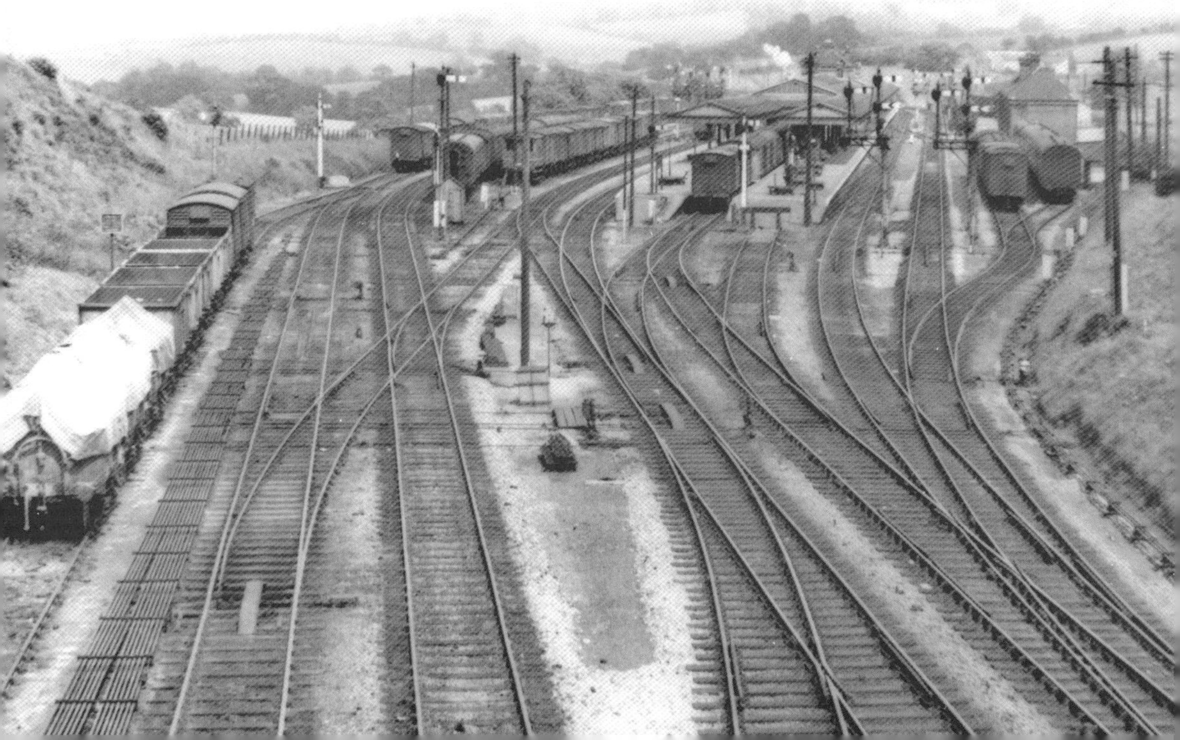

93. No. 47554 heads the 11.07 Penzance to Manchester on 2nd July 1977. The road vehicles are on the site of the previous station. The 163-lever Station South box was on the right (out of view) until 8th October 1979. (T.Heavyside)

94.	No. 6000 *King George V* is arriving with a special from Newport to Shrewsbury on the same day. By that time the once impressive station had been decimated. The railings are around the subway stairwell. (T.Heavyside)

95.	Departing on 14th August 1984 is no. 33018 with the 12.30 Manchester to Cardiff, formed of five Mk. I coaches. The main building was demolished later, leaving only a hole in the embankment as access to the subway under the down line. The platforms were shortened to eliminate all trace of the bays and "Road" was dropped from the name on 1st May 1972. The siding was retained by the engineers into the 21st century. (D.H.Mitchell)

SOUTH OF PONTYPOOL ROAD

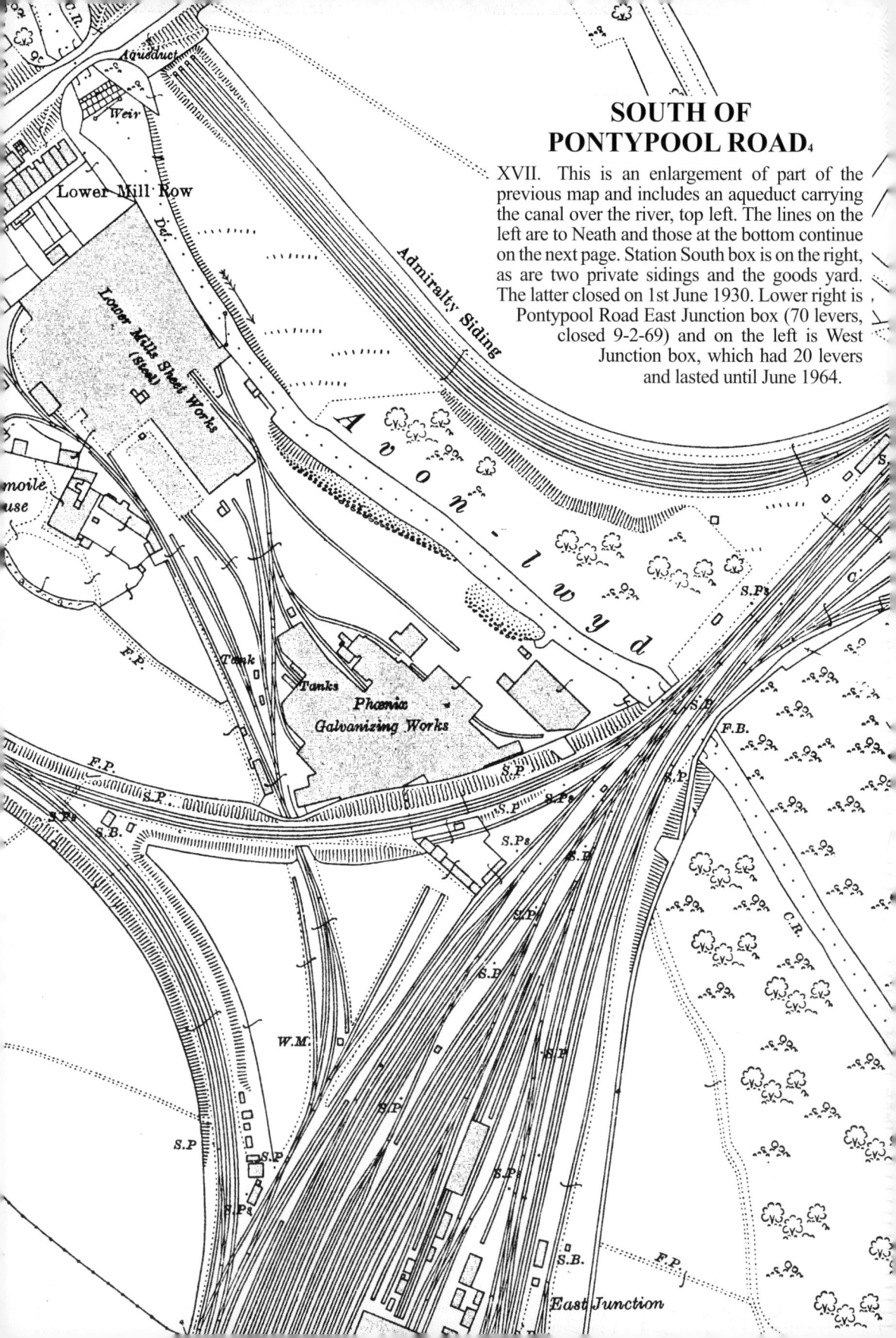

XVII. This is an enlargement of part of the previous map and includes an aqueduct carrying the canal over the river, top left. The lines on the left are to Neath and those at the bottom continue on the next page. Station South box is on the right, as are two private sidings and the goods yard. The latter closed on 1st June 1930. Lower right is Pontypool Road East Junction box (70 levers, closed 9-2-69) and on the left is West Junction box, which had 20 levers and lasted until June 1964.

XVIII. The eight-road engine shed closed in May 1965. To the left of it is Middle Junction box (40 levers, closed by 1943) and to the left of the goods shed is South Junction box (46 levers, closed 5-9-65).

96. The shed was coded 86G and its south end was photographed on 21st July 1963. It opened in 1869 or 1879, records conflict; the latter date probably refers to the roundhouse section. There was an allocation of 87 locomotives, plus one diesel railcar, in December 1947. (C.L.Caddy)

97. There was access to only three of the eight roads at the north end, as seen on 13th July 1958. One line ran onto the turntable of the roundhouse. No. 5638 is one of the 5600 class introduced by the GWR in 1924. On the right is the high level line of the coal stage, which is marked near the bottom of map XVII. (H.C.Casserley)

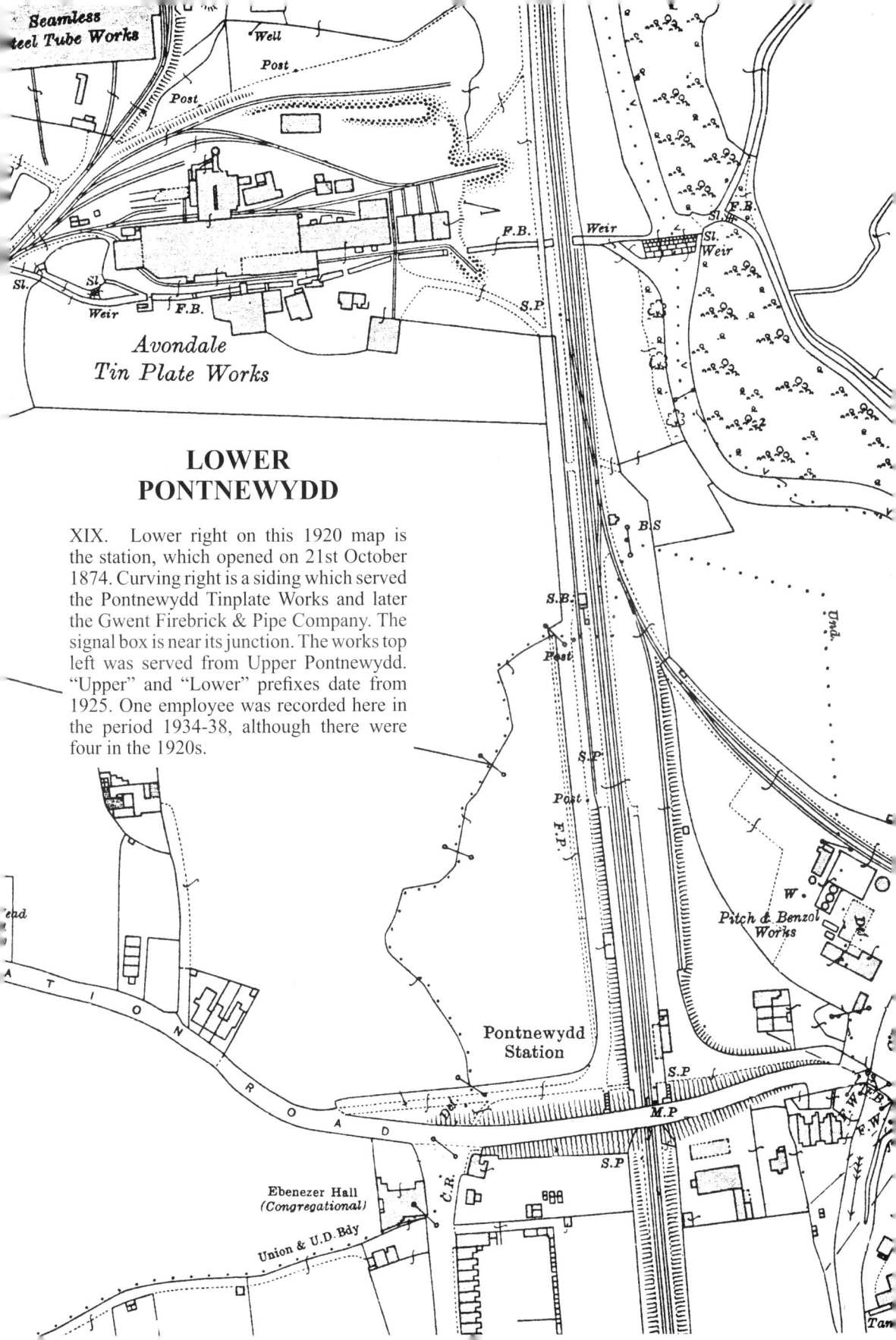

LOWER PONTNEWYDD

XIX. Lower right on this 1920 map is the station, which opened on 21st October 1874. Curving right is a siding which served the Pontnewydd Tinplate Works and later the Gwent Firebrick & Pipe Company. The signal box is near its junction. The works top left was served from Upper Pontnewydd. "Upper" and "Lower" prefixes date from 1925. One employee was recorded here in the period 1934-38, although there were four in the 1920s.

98. Passenger service was withdrawn on 9th June 1958, but goods lasted until 25th January 1965. There had been a temporary closure during World War I. In the distance in this photo from 8th August 1961 is the 21-lever signal box, which functioned until 27th September 1965. (M.Hale)

Lower Pontnewydd	1903	1913	1923	1932
Passenger tickets issued	17866	19117	23142	3525
Season tickets issued	*	*	141	46
Parcels forwarded	1495	1601	1257	765
General goods forwarded (tons)	451	5030	934	2086
Coal and coke received (tons)	2591	4242	1404	146
Other minerals received (tons)	1797	4439	13098	11489
General goods received (tons)	330	2590	763	259
Trucks of livestock handled	-	-	-	-

(* not available.)

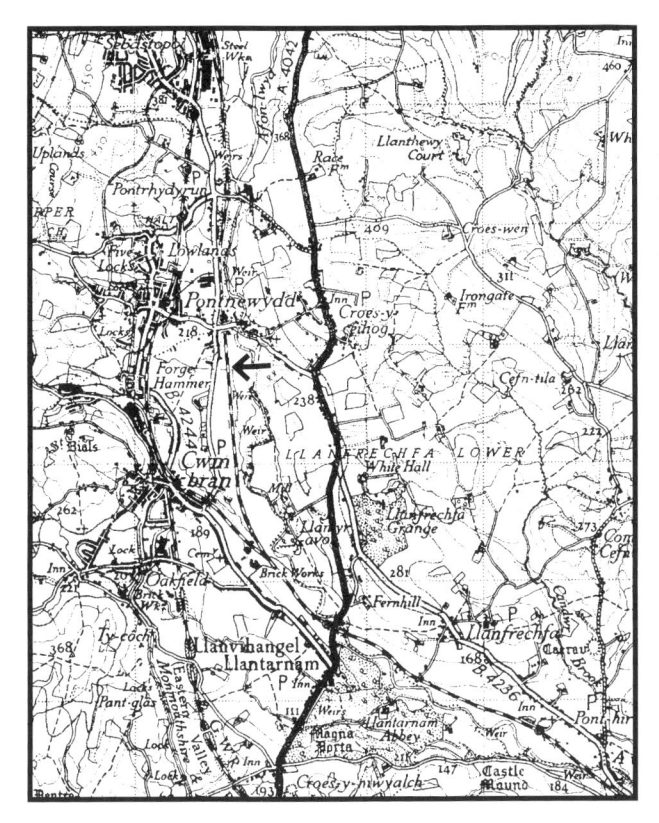

CWMBRAN

XX. The area has been extensively developed and a new station was opened on 12th May 1986. Its approximate position is arrowed on this 1ins to 1 mile survey of 1946. The old station is below the words "Cwm bran".

99. This northward view is from soon after the opening of the station. The initial down service comprised 12 weekday trains, with three on Sundays. (Lens of Sutton coll.)

XXI. The 1922 extract at 6ins to 1 mile has our route top centre and Llantarnam station on the right. It opened in August 1878. Top left is the original Cwmbran station, on the 1878 link line. An up goods loop was added between Llantarnam and Llantarnam Junction in December 1914 and a down one followed in November 1941. The former was removed in March 1964, but the latter lasted until 8th June 1980. The signal box shown at the station had 23 levers, but only a nine-lever ground frame remained after July 1933, this lasting until May 1956.

Llantarnam	1903	1913	1923	1932
Passenger tickets issued	24571	29358	28504	4834
Season tickets issued	*	*	335	51
Parcels forwarded	2025	2692	1236	1275
General goods forwarded (tons)	774	1358	1419	1496
Coal and coke received (tons)	7746	8375	5066	874
Other minerals received (tons)	2353	4632	5355	3874
General goods received (tons)	806	941	1035	391
Trucks of livestock handled	2	6	29	16

(* not available.)

100. An undated postcard includes the goods shed in the distance. There were ten men recorded here in 1923, but the figure had dropped to four during the following ten years. (J.Langford coll.)

101. A southbound freight rattles through on 31st March 1961, hauled by 0-6-2T no. 6690. In the distance is the goods yard, which closed on 7th September 1963. (J.Langford)

102. A panorama from the footbridge on the same day includes the factory of Weston's Biscuits, which had a private siding between 1938 and about 1977. Local passenger service was withdrawn on 30th April 1962. (J.Langford)

103. Llantarnam Junction box had 46 levers and was in use from 1913 to 29th November 1983. The down goods loop had passed behind the box, which was photographed in about 1969. (R.D.Wittamore/Kidderminster Railway Museum)

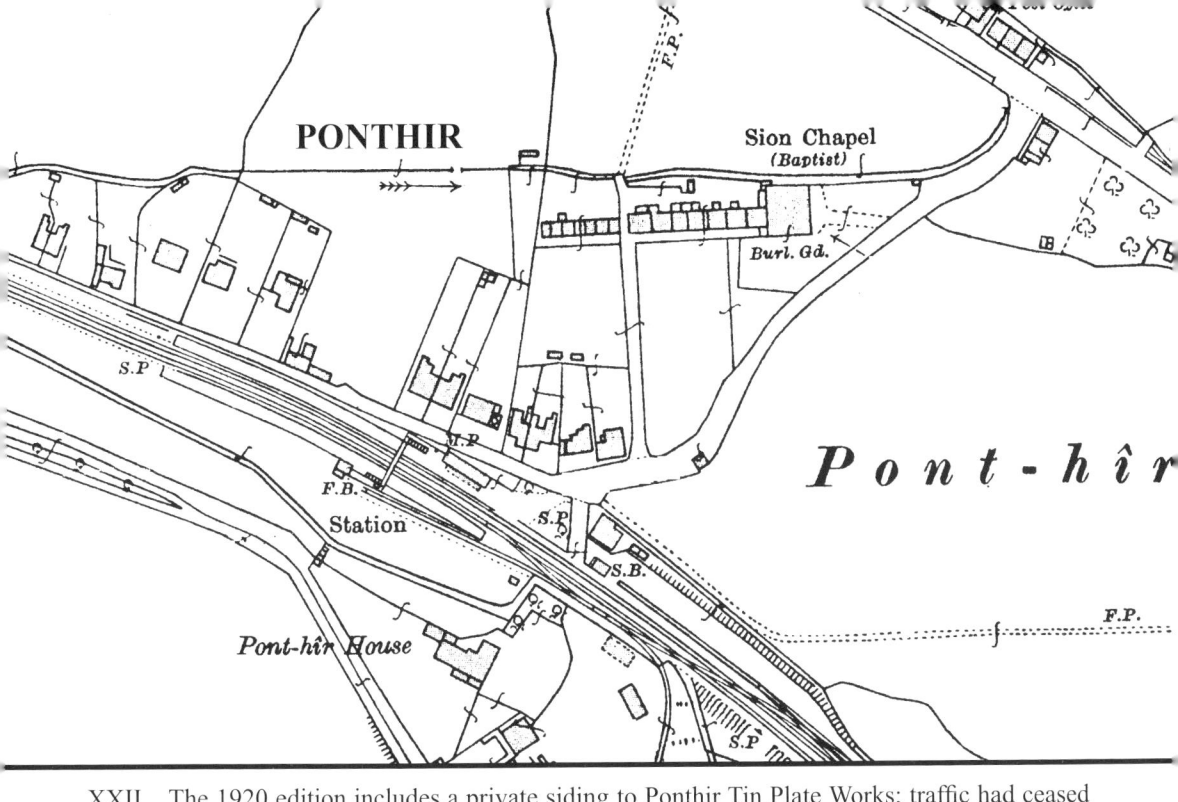

XXII. The 1920 edition includes a private siding to Ponthir Tin Plate Works; traffic had ceased by that time. The station opened four years after this part of the route, on 1st June 1878. The signal box was in use from about 1885 until 20th August 1961; there were 20 levers.

104. This is a 1962 view towards Newport. There were three men here for most of the 1930s. Passenger service lasted until 30th April 1962, but goods traffic ceased on 9th May 1958. The house in the left background still stands; it is believed to have been the stationmaster's residence. (Stations UK)

CAERLEON

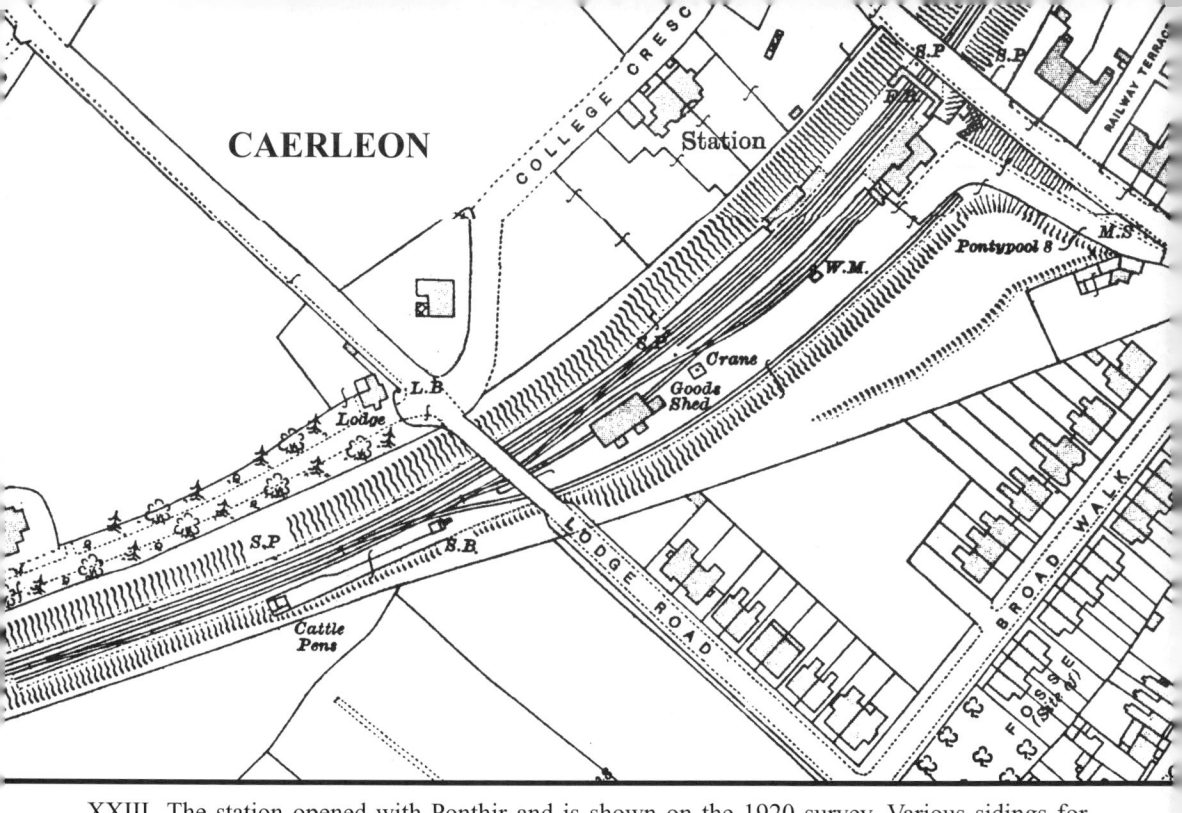

XXIII. The station opened with Ponthir and is shown on the 1920 survey. Various sidings for Caerleon Tin Works were provided about ¼ mile to the north from around 1880 to 1963. A signal box with 29 levers was in place there until 1952. The one on this map had opened by 1885.

105. This view of a northbound train is thought to date from about 1905, at a time when there were about a dozen men employed here. (Lens of Sutton coll.)

106. This indelibly dated photograph gives a good impression of the busy goods yard, which was later provided with a 30cwt crane. The goods shed was still standing in 2005. (Lens of Sutton coll.)

107. This 1935 view is towards Hereford. The buildings survive largely, albeit somewhat altered. Passenger traffic ceased on 30th April 1962, although the town had grown from 1367 in 1901 to 4870 in 1961. (Stations UK)

108. Until August 1961, there was a 23-lever signal box; it is in the distance, on the right. The goods yard closed on 29th November 1965; the photo dates from 1962. (Stations UK)

EAST OF NEWPORT

XXIV. Our route is top right on this 1947 survey at 6ins to 1 mile. It joins the London to Cardiff line at the triangular Maindee Junction, before crossing the River Usk to enter the main station, usually known as "High Street". Top right is a smaller bridge over the Usk, known as St Julian's, and south of it was a siding to the brickworks prior to 1930. South of Maindee North Junction, there are still four parallel tracks, although the 49-lever box closed on 28th May 1962. Many through trains between the West and North of England once used East Loop regularly. Engineers sidings are inside the triangle, but are now accessed from the north.

109. The first bridge over the Usk was a wooden affair and part of it was damaged by fire before carrying a train. A wrought iron structure followed in 1886, its bowstring span being seen in this 1924 picture, shortly before replacement by steel lattice components each weighing 52 tons. (GWR Magazine)

110. Quadrupling also took place in 1924 and the resulting bridge was photographed on 3rd July 1977 as no. 6000 *King George V* returned to Shrewsbury on its 50th anniversary run. (T.Heavyside)

NEWPORT

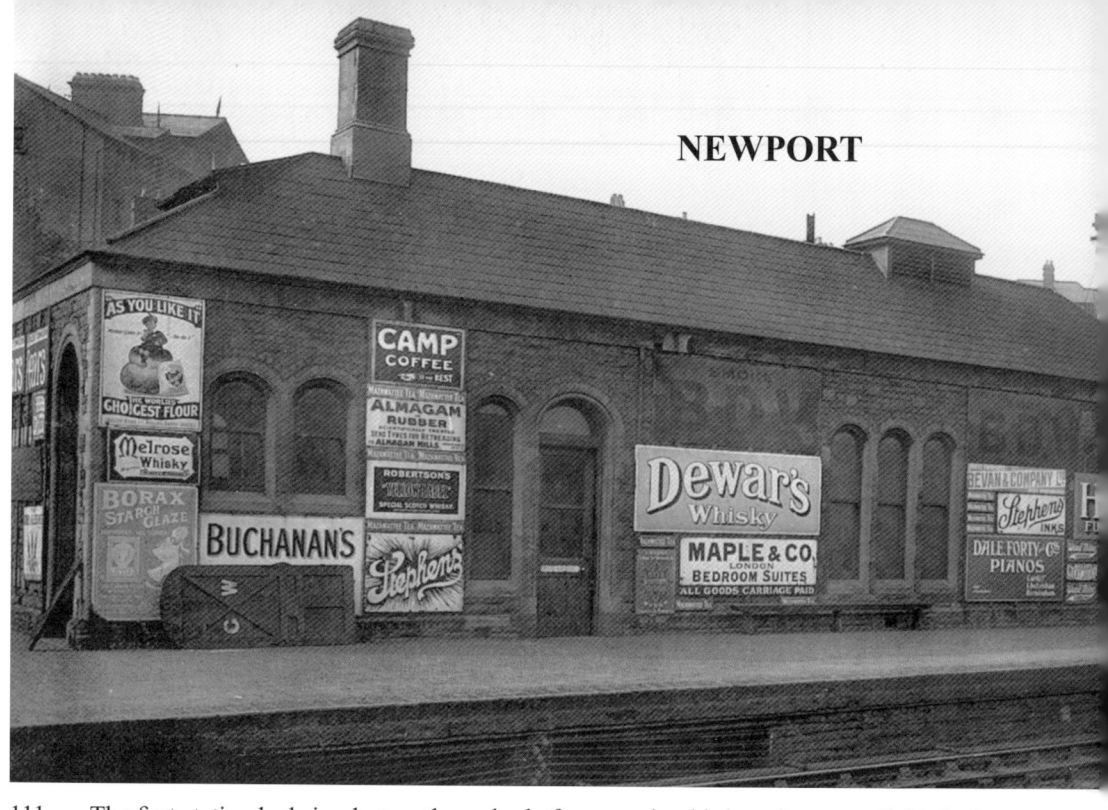

111. The first station had simply two through platforms and a third track was available before broad gauge was abandoned. In 1880, the station was redesigned with new buildings, an additional through platform and a bay, together with two tracks for non-stop trains. The long platform was recorded in 1913, along with evidence of an over-zealous advertising agent. (GWR)

(lower left) 112. The Brecon & Methyr Railway also used the station and their no. 18 was photographed at the down platform on 24th July 1905. It became GWR no. 1460. In 1923, there was a staff of 244 on passenger duties and 271 on goods. (K.Nunn/LCGB)

XXV. The rebuilding of the station lasted from 1923 until 1930, the booking hall on the down side being the last part to be completed. The GWR published this plan in June 1930. The left footbridge was retained.

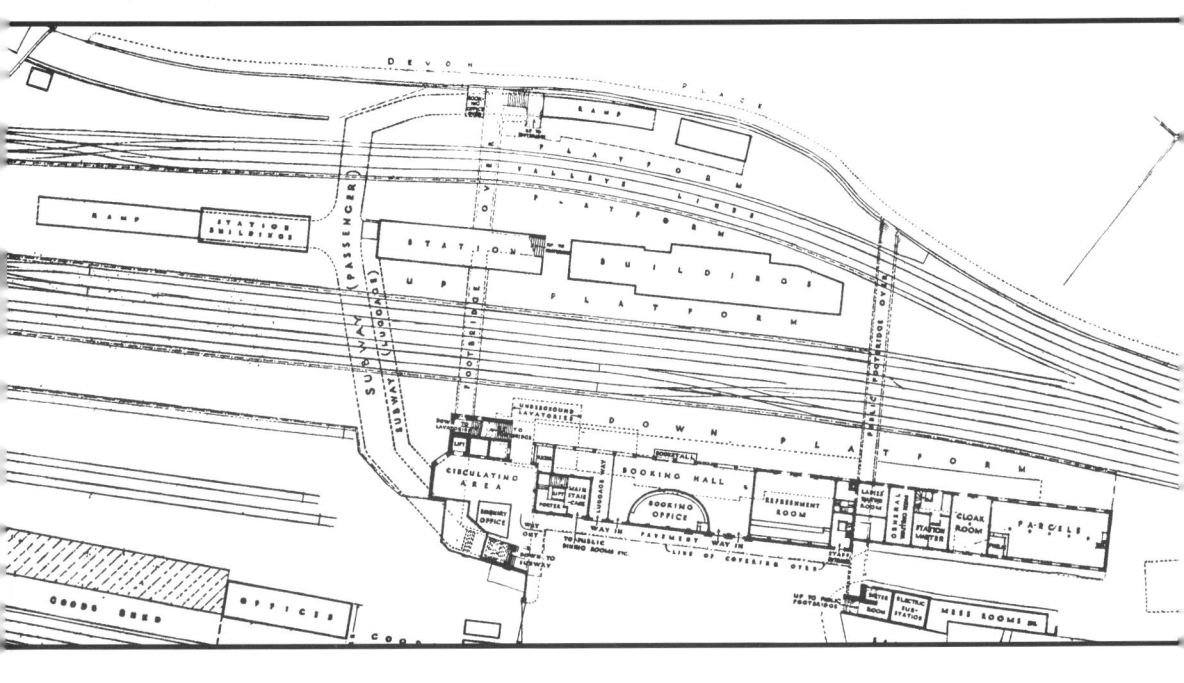

113. The dining room was on the first floor and would seat 200, surrounded by Japanese oak panelling. This establishment would account for some of the "passenger" staff.
(GWR Magazine)

114. The northern platforms were usually used by trains for the Valleys. Standing at no. 8 on 27th August 1931 are GWR 0-6-0PT no. 7776 and LMS 0-6-2T no. 7822. No. 8 was created during further alterations in 1926-28.
(M.J.Stretton coll.)

115. Running west on 10th May 1954 on the down main line is 0-6-2T no. 6608. The track to the right of the train was described as "down platform" at that time. The former was termed "down relief" later. (T.J.Edgington)

116. No. 7771 is standing at platform 8 on 25th July 1958. The platforms were renumbered on 16th April 1961, this becoming no. 1; the main up platform was 5 and the down one was 6.
(G.Adams/M.J.Stretton coll.)

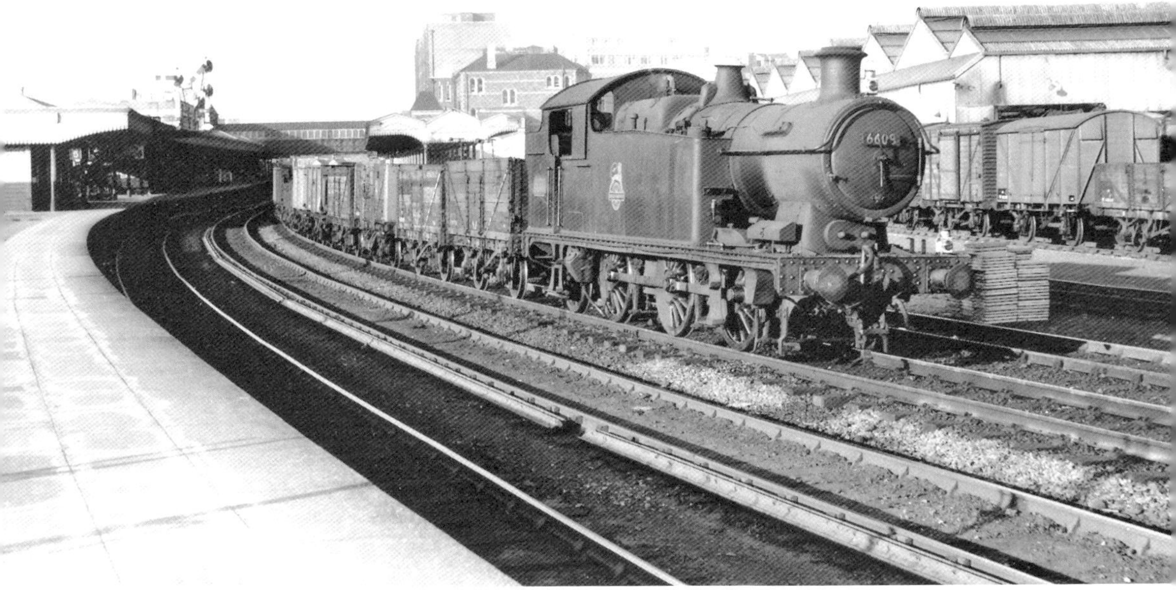

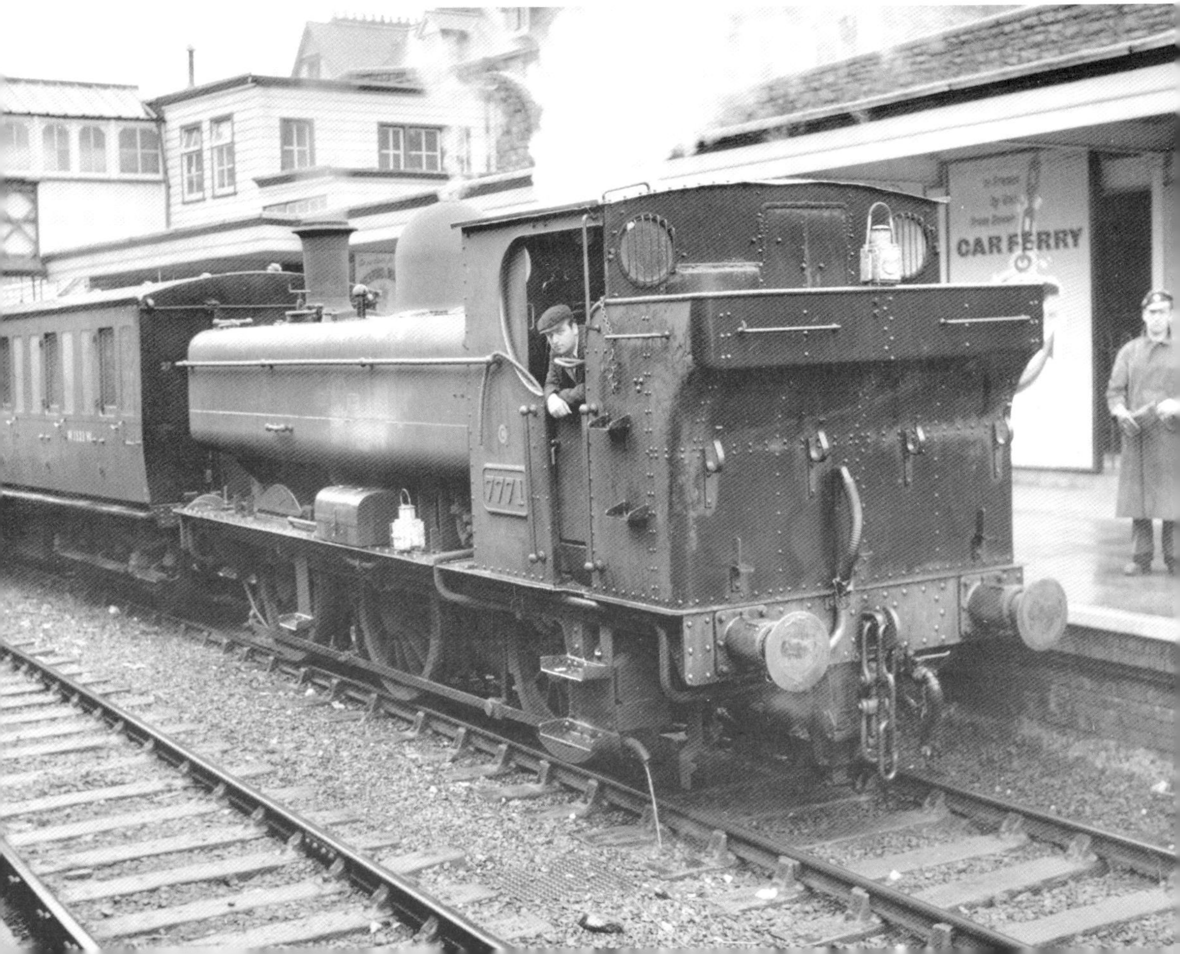
CAR FERRY
7771

117. This is the view towards the Usk bridge from platform 4 in the 1950s and until Newport Panel came into use beyond the right border of the picture on 9th December 1962. In the distance is East Box which closed that day, having opened in 1927. (D.B.Clayton)

118. Further renumbering resulted in the down platform (right) becoming no. 1 and to be little used. No. 1015 *Western Champion* is with a down train at platform 2. Up trains mostly use no. 3 and there is a through line north of it. All three are reversible, as is the up relief. (R.E.Toop)

119. No. 37228 is on the down relief line with coal empties on 19th October 1979. Parcels have priority on platform 1. A footbridge over the two northern tracks from the car park to the island platform was provided later. (D.H.Mitchell)

120. Platform 1 is deserted in this view from 27th September 2000 as a down class 158 calls on its way to Cardiff. The choice of destinations and train frequencies is at its highest, but sadly airline sardine packing principles have been employed by recent train designers too often. (F.Hornby)

Other views of this station can be found in our *Brecon to Newport* and *Swindon to Newport* albums.

Middleton Press

EVOLVING THE ULTIMATE RAIL ENCYCLOPEDIA

Easebourne Lane, Midhurst, West Sussex.
GU29 9AZ Tel:01730 813169
www.middletonpress.co.uk email:info@middletonpress.co.uk
A-0 906520   B-1 873793   C-1 901706   D-1 904474

OOP Out of Print at time of printing - Please check current availability   **BROCHURE AVAILABLE SHOWING NEW TITLES**

A
Abergavenny to Merthyr C 91 5
Aldgate & Stepney Tramways B 70 7
Allhallows - Branch Line to A 62 2
Alton - Branch Lines to A 11 8
Andover to Southampton A 82 7
Ascot - Branch Lines around A 64 9
Ashburton - Branch Line to B 95 2
Ashford - Steam to Eurostar B 67 7
Ashford to Dover A 48 7
Austrian Narrow Gauge D 04 7
Avonmouth - BL around D 42 X

B
Banbury to Birmingham D 27 6
Barking to Southend C 80 X
Barnet & Finchley Tramways B 93 6
Barry - BL around D 50 0
Basingstoke to Salisbury A 89 4
Bath Green Park to Bristol C 36 2
Bath to Evercreech Junction A 60 6
Bath Tramways B 86 3
Battle over Portsmouth 1940 A 29 0
Battle over Sussex 1940 A 79 7
Bedford to Wellingborough D 31 4
Betwixt Petersfield & Midhurst A 94 0
Blitz over Sussex 1941-42 B 35 9
Bodmin - Branch Lines around B 83 9
Bognor at War 1939-45 B 59 6
Bombers over Sussex 1943-45 B 51 0
Bournemouth & Poole Trys B 47 2 OOP
Bournemouth to Evercreech Jn A 46 0
Bournemouth to Weymouth A 57 6
Bournemouth Trolleybuses C 10 9
Bradford Trolleybuses D 19 5
Brecon to Neath D 43 8
Brecon to Newport D 16 0
Brickmaking in Sussex B 19 7
Brightons Tramways B 02 2
Brighton to Eastbourne A 16 9
Brighton to Worthing A 03 7
Bristols Tramways B 57 X
Bristol to Taunton D 03 9
Bromley South to Rochester B 23 5 OOP
Bude - Branch Line to B 29 4
Burnham to Evercreech Jn A 68 1
Burton & Ashby Tramways C 51 6

C
Camberwell & West Norwood Tys B 22 7
Cambridge to Ely EML 55 1
Canterbury - Branch Lines around B 58 8
Caterham & Tattenham Corner B 25 1
Changing Midhurst C 15 X
Chard and Yeovil - BLs around C 30 3
Charing Cross to Dartford A 75 4
Charing Cross to Orpington A 96 7
Cheddar - Branch Line to B 90 1
Cheltenham to Andover C 43 5
Chesterfield Tramways D 37 3
Chesterfield Trolleybuses D 51 9
Chichester to Portsmouth A 14 2 OOP
Clapham & Streatham Tramways B 97 9
Clapham Junction - 50 yrs C 06 0
Clapham Junction to Beckenham Jn B 36 7
Clevedon & Portishead - BLs to D 18 7
Collectors Trains, Trolleys & Trams D 29 2
Cornwall Narrow Gauge D 56 X
Crawley to Littlehampton A 34 7
Cromer - Branch Lines around C 26 5
Croydons Tramways B 42 5
Croydons Trolleybuses B 73 1 OOP
Croydon to East Grinstead B 48 0
Crystal Palace (HL) & Catford Loop A 87 8

D
Darlington Trolleybuses D 33 0
Dartford to Sittingbourne B 34 0
Derby Tramways D 17 9
Derby Trolleybuses C 72 9
Derwent Valley - Branch Line to the D 06 3
Didcot to Banbury D 02 0
Didcot to Swindon C 84 2
Didcot to Winchester C 13 3
Douglas to Peel C 88 5
Douglas to Port Erin C 55 9
Douglas to Ramsey D 39 X
Dover's Tramways B 24 3
Dover to Ramsgate A 78 9

E
Ealing to Slough C 42 7
Eastbourne to Hastings A 27 4
East Cornwall Mineral Railways D 22 5
East Croydon to Three Bridges A 53 3
East Grinstead - Branch Lines to A 07 X
East Ham & West Ham Tramways B 52 9
East Kent Light Railway A 61 4
East London - Branch Lines of C 44 3
East London Line B 80 4
East Ridings Secret Resistance D 21 7
Edgware & Willesden Tramways C 18 4
Effingham Junction - BLs around A 74 6
Eltham & Woolwich Tramways B 74 X
Ely to Kings Lynn C 53 2
Ely to Norwich C 90 7
Embankment & Waterloo Tramways B 41 3
Enfield & Wood Green Trys C 03 6 OOP
Enfield Town & Palace Gates - BL to D 32 2
Epsom to Horsham A 30 4
Euston to Harrow & Wealdstone C 89 3
Exeter & Taunton Tramways B 32 4
Exeter to Barnstaple B 15 2
Exeter to Newton Abbot C 49 4
Exeter to Tavistock B 69 3
Exmouth - Branch Lines to B 00 6 OOP

F
Fairford - Branch Line to A 52 5
Falmouth, Helston & St. Ives - BL to C 74 5
Fareham to Salisbury A 67 3
Faversham to Dover B 05 7 OOP
Felixstowe & Aldeburgh - BL to D 20 9
Fenchurch Street to Barking C 20 6
Festiniog - 50 yrs of enterprise C 83 4
Festiniog in the Fifties B 68 5
Festiniog in the Sixties B 91 X
Finsbury Park to Alexandra Palace C 02 8
Frome to Bristol B 77 4
Fulwell - Trams, Trolleys & Buses D 11 X

G
Garraway Father & Son A 20 7 OOP
Gloucester to Bristol D 35 7
Gosport & Horndean Trys B 92 8 OOP
Gosport - Branch Lines around A 36 3
Great Yarmouth Tramways D 13 6
Greenwich & Dartford Tramways B 14 6 OOP
Guildford to Redhill A 63 0

H
Hammersmith & Hounslow Trys C 33 8
Hampshire Narrow Gauge D 36 5
Hampshire Waterways A 84 3 OOP
Hampstead & Highgate Tramways B 53 7
Harrow to Watford D 14 4
Hastings to Ashford A 37 1 OOP
Hastings Tramways B 18 9 OOP
Hastings Trolleybuses B 81 2 OOP
Hawkhurst - Branch Line to A 66 5
Hayling - Branch Line to A 12 6
Haywards Heath to Seaford A 28 2 OOP
Henley, Windsor & Marlow - BL to C 77 X
Hereford to Newport WML D 54 3
Hitchin to Peterborough D 07 1
Holborn & Finsbury Tramways B 79 0
Holborn Viaduct to Lewisham A 81 9
Horsham - Branch Lines to A 02 9
Huddersfield Trolleybuses C 92 3
Hull Trolleybuses D 24 1
Huntingdon - Branch Lines around A 93 2

I
Ilford & Barking Tramways B 61 8
Ilford to Shenfield C 97 4
Ilfracombe - Branch Line to B 21 9
Ilkeston & Glossop Tramways D 40 3
Industrial Rlys of the South East A 09 6
Ipswich to Saxmundham C 41 9/8 OOP
Isle of Wight Lines - 50 yrs C 12 5

K
Kent & East Sussex Waterways A 72 X
Kent Narrow Gauge C 45 1
Kingsbridge - Branch Line to C 98 2
Kingston & Hounslow Loops A 83 5
Kingston & Wimbledon Tramways B 56 1
Kingswear - Branch Line to C 17 6

L
Lambourn - Branch Line to C 70 2
Launceston & Princetown - BL to C 19 2
Lewisham & Catford Tramways B 26 X OOP
Lewisham to Dartford A 92 4
Lines around Wimbledon B 75 8
Liverpool Street to Chingford D 01 2

Liverpool Street to Ilford C 34 6
Liverpool Tramways - Eastern C 04 4
Liverpool Tramways - Northern C 46 X
Liverpool Tramways - Southern C 23 0
London Bridge to Addiscombe B 20 0 OOP
London Bridge to East Croydon A 58 4
London Chatham & Dover Railway A 88 6
London Termini - Past and Proposed D 00 4
London to Portsmouth Waterways B 43 X
Longmoor - Branch Lines to A 41 X
Looe - Branch Line to C 22 2
Lyme Regis - Branch Line to A 45 2
Lynton - Branch Line to B 04 9

M
Maidstone & Chatham Tramways B 40 5
Maidstone Trolleybuses C 00 1 OOP
March - Branch Lines around B 09 X
Margate & Ramsgate Tramways C 52 4
Marylebone to Rickmansworth D 49 7
Midhurst - Branch Lines around A 49 5
Midhurst - Branch Lines to A 01 0 OOP
Military Defence of West Sussex A 23 1
Military Signals, South Coast C 54 0
Minehead - Branch Line to A 80 0
Mitcham Junction Lines B 01 4
Mitchell & company C 59 1
Moreton-in-Marsh to Worcester D 26 8
Moretonhampstead - Branch Line to C 27 3

N
Newbury to Westbury C 66 4
Newport - Branch Lines to A 26 6
Newquay - Branch Lines to C 71 0
Newton Abbot to Plymouth C 60 5
Northern France Narrow Gauge C 75 3
North East German Narrow Gauge D 44 6
North Kent Tramways B 44 8
North London Line B 94 4
North Woolwich - BLs around C 65 6
Norwich Tramways C 40 0
Nottinghamshire & Derbyshire Tramway D 53 5

O
Orpington to Tonbridge B 03 0
Oxford to Moreton-in-Marsh D 15 2

P
Paddington to Ealing C 37 0
Paddington to Princes Risborough C 81 8
Padstow - Branch Line to B 54 5
Plymouth - BLs around B 98 7
Plymouth to St. Austell C 63 X
Porthmadog 1954-94 - BL around B 31 6
Porthmadog to Blaenau B 50 2 OOP
Portmadoc 1923-46 - BL around B 13 8
Portsmouths Tramways B 72 3 OOP
Portsmouth to Southampton A 31 2
Portsmouth Trolleybuses C 73 7
Princes Risborough - Branch Lines to D 05 5
Princes Risborough to Banbury C 85 0

R
Railways to Victory C 16 8/7 OOP
Reading to Basingstoke B 27 8
Reading to Didcot C 79 6
Reading to Guildford A 47 9 OOP
Reading Tramways B 87 1
Reading Trolleybuses C 05 2
Redhill to Ashford A 73 8
Return to Blaenau 1970-82 C 64 8
Roman Roads of Surrey C 61 3
Roman Roads of Sussex C 48 6
Romneyrail C 32 X
Ryde to Ventnor A 19 3

S
Salisbury to Westbury B 39 1
Salisbury to Yeovil B 06 5
Saxmundham to Yarmouth C 69 9
Saxony Narrow Gauge D 47 0
Seaton & Eastbourne T/Ws B 76 6 OOP
Seaton & Sidmouth - Branch Lines to A 95 9
Secret Sussex Resistance B 82 0
SECR Centenary album C 11 7
Selsey - Branch Line to A 04 5 OOP
Sheerness - Branch Lines around B 16 2
Shepherds Bush to Uxbridge T/Ws C 28 1
Shrewsbury - Branch Line to A 86 X
Sierra Leone Narrow Gauge D 28 4
Sittingbourne to Ramsgate A 90 8
Slough to Newbury C 56 7
Solent - Creeks, Crafts & Cargoes D 52 7

Southamptons Tramways B 33 2 OOP
Southampton to Bournemouth A 42 8
Southend-on-Sea Tramways B 28 6
Southern France Narrow Gauge C 47 8
Southwark & Deptford Tramways B 38 3
Southwold - Branch Line to A 15 0
South Eastern & Chatham Railways C 08 ?
South London Line B 46 4
South London Tramways 1903-33 D 10 1
St. Albans to Bedford D 08 X
St. Austell to Penzance C 67 2
St. Pancras to St. Albans C 78 8
Stamford Hill Tramways B 85 5
Steaming through Cornwall B 30 8
Steaming through Kent A 13 4 OOP
Steaming through the Isle of Wight A 56 8
Steaming through West Hants A 69 X
Stratford-upon-Avon to Cheltenham C 25 ?
Strood to Paddock Wood B 12 X
Surrey Home Guard C 57 5
Surrey Narrow Gauge C 87 7
Surrey Waterways A 51 7 OOP
Sussex Home Guard C 24 9
Sussex Narrow Gauge C 68 0
Sussex Shipping Sail, Steam & Motor D 23 ?
Swanley to Ashford B 45 6
Swindon to Bristol C 96 6
Swindon to Gloucester D 46 2
Swindon to Newport D 30 6
Swiss Narrow Gauge C 94 X

T
Talyllyn - 50 years C 39 7
Taunton to Barnstaple B 60 X
Taunton to Exeter C 82 6
Tavistock to Plymouth B 88 X
Tees-side Trolleybuses D 58 6
Tenterden - Branch Line to A 21 5
Thanet's Tramways B 11 1 OOP
Three Bridges to Brighton A 35 5
Tilbury Loop C 86 9
Tiverton - Branch Lines around C 62 1
Tivetshall to Beccles D 41 1
Tonbridge to Hastings A 44 4
Torrington - Branch Lines to B 37 5
Tunbridge Wells - Branch Lines to A 32 0
Twickenham & Kingston Trys C 35 4
Two-Foot Gauge Survivors C 21 4 OOP

U
Upwell - Branch Line to B 64 2

V
Victoria & Lambeth Tramways B 49 9
Victoria to Bromley South A 98 3
Victoria to East Croydon A 40 1
Vivarais C 31 1

W
Walthamstow & Leyton Tramways B 65 0
Waltham Cross & Edmonton Trys C 07 9
Wandsworth & Battersea Tramways B 63 ?
Wantage - Branch Line to D 25 X
Wareham to Swanage - 50 yrs D 09 8
War on the Line A 10 X
War on the Line VIDEO + 88 0
Waterloo to Windsor A 54 1
Waterloo to Woking A 38 X OOP
Watford to Leighton Buzzard D 45 4
Wenford Bridge to Fowey C 09 5
Westbury to Bath B 55 3
Westbury to Taunton C 76 1
West Cornwall Mineral Railways D 48 9
West Croydon to Epsom B 08 1
West London - Branch Lines of C 50 8
West London Line B 84 7
West Sussex Waterways A 24 X
West Wiltshire - Branch Lines of D 12 8
Weymouth - Branch Lines around A 65 7 O
Willesden Junction to Richmond B 71 5
Wimbledon to Beckenham C 58 3
Wimbledon to Epsom B 62 6
Wimborne - Branch Lines around A 97 5
Wisbech - Branch Lines around C 01 X
Wisbech 1800-1901 C 93 1
Woking to Alton A 59 2
Woking to Portsmouth A 25 8
Woking to Southampton A 55 X
Woolwich & Dartford Trolleys B 66 9 OOP
Worcester to Hereford D 38 1
Worthing to Chichester A 06 1 OOP

Y
Yeovil - 50 yrs change C 38 9
Yeovil to Dorchester A 76 2
Yeovil to Exeter A 91 6

96